£6·40

JANUA LINGUARUM

STUDIA MEMORIAE
NICOLAI VAN WIJK DEDICATA

edenda curat

C. H. VAN SCHOONEVELD

Indiana University

Series Minor, 154

ONE WORD AT A TIME

The use of single word utterances
before syntax

by

LOIS BLOOM

Teachers College, Columbia University

Third Printing

1976
MOUTON
THE HAGUE · PARIS

First Printing 1973
Second Printing 1975

LIBRARY OF CONGRESS CATALOG CARD NUMBER: 72-94445

ISBN 90 279 3375 8

Printed in The Netherlands

PREFACE

"The many biographical studies of the child study movement around the turn of the century were replete with isolated observations of the language of single children who were for the most part precocious and observed by biased relatives under varying conditions" — a statement by Dorothea McCarthy in 1950 that seemed to represent the view that prevailed from the 1930s through the 1950s of earlier child language studies[1]. It is abundantly clear, as we enter the 1970s, that the enigma of language development and the problems of studying child language endure — in spite of what we have learned since the turn of the century. This study was motivated by questions that have emerged gradually out of the child language studies that have come before it. In particular, the psycholinguistic studies of the last decade have led to hypotheses about the origin of early grammar which may now be tested by renewed extended observations of presyntax speech. And so, another diary account. A substantial portion of the data reported here was obtained through observations of a single child, who was precocious, and who was observed by a biased relative under varying conditions. However, the use of video tape recording resulted in a body of data that could be confirmed by other investigators, and these data are included in this report (as an Appendix) for that purpose.

In the fall and spring of 1969-70 I was teaching a seminar in language development at Teachers College, Columbia University.

[1] Dorothea McCarthy, Language development. In *Encyclopedia of Research*, 1950, pp. 165-172.

At that time my daughter Allison was between her first and second birthdays, and her speech, as reported from my notes and recorded on video tape, was the subject of lively and intense debate. In large part, it was those weekly seminar sessions that stimulated the study reported here. I am grateful to Margaret Lahey, Lorraine Harner, Daphne Fox, Doris Allen, Suzanne Embree, Richard Sanders and Tory Higgins (the members of the seminar), for their probing questions and comments which contributed to many of the ideas that have been developed here. I am indebted to Lois Hood, for her careful initial transcription of the Allison video tapes and to Patsy Lightbown, Maxine Kenin and Lynn Streeter, who verified the accuracy of the original transcriptions, and to all four for their care in listening, watching, analyzing, and counting; to Leo Yam, who was producer and photographer for the video tape sessions; and to Debra Franco, for her cool at the typewriter.

The research was supported in part by Research Grant HD 03828 from the National Institute of Child Health and Human Development, and in part by Fellowship No. 5-FI-MH-30,001 from the National Institute of Mental Health, The United States Public Health Service. A number of people have been kind enough to give me their comments and criticisms after reading a first draft of this manuscript, and I am pleased to acknowledge my appreciation to them here: Melissa Bowerman, Peter R. Carey, William G. Hardy, Janellen Huttenlocher, David Ingram, William Labov, David Mc-Neill, David Palermo, and Susan Weiner. An early version of this monograph was presented to the Eastern Verbal Investigators League at Princeton, New Jersey, October 1970. A portion of this monograph was presented to the Conference on Developmental Psycholinguistics at the Linguistic Society of America Summer Institute, University of Buffalo, August 1971.

I am especially grateful to three very important people in Allison's life — Olga Stone, Marie Bauza (Mimi) and my husband, Robert H. Bloom. And, of course, the dedication of this book is to Allison, my daughter.

TABLE OF CONTENTS

LIST OF TABLES

1

THE PROBLEM AND THE DATA

Virtually all children go through a fairly long period, at least several months, in which they utter only one word at a time, before they begin to use syntax in their speech. Once children begin to combine two words it is possible to begin, with some confidence, to describe and attempt to explain the emergence of grammar. But how does the child arrive at his first linguistic notions of grammar? We know that children are not actively 'taught' rules of grammar; they must somehow discover the special relationship between the form of the speech that they hear and particular aspects of their experience. There is little doubt that this discovery procedure has its beginnings when children begin to talk — to use single-word utterances — if not before.

With the introduction of generative transformational grammar in the late 1950s it appeared as though an account of the underlying productivity of children's early sentences might be possible. Research in child language in the 1960s moved almost exclusively in that direction[1]. These studies DESCRIBED the emergence of grammar in the speech of a small group of children, and have shed some light on the nature of early sentences and what two-year-old children appear to know about grammar. Most EXPLANATIONS of the emergence of grammar that have been offered — based not

---

[1] Martin D. S. Braine, "The ontogeny of English phrase structure: the first phase", *Language*, 1963; Ursula Bellugi and Roger Brown (eds.), *The acquisition of language*, monograph of the Society for Research in Child Development, 1964; David McNeill, "Developmental psycholinguistics", in Frank Smith and George A. Miller (eds.), *The genesis of language*, 1966, 15-84; and Lois Bloom, *Language development: Form and function in emerging grammars*, 1968; 1970.

only upon the handful of studies in the last decade but on the studies of child language in the last half century — have placed considerable emphasis on children's linguistic experience. It has generally been assumed that the child needs to induce the system of rules which underlies all of the many and different sentences that are possible in his language by listening to only those sentences he hears in his first few years. Moreover there has been a strong inclination towards viewing the period of single-word utterances as a single stage of development in which the child needs primarily to learn the meanings of words, to acquire a lexicon. Most investigators have credited children with considerably more knowledge of sentences than is manifested in their early speech, that is, in the use of single-word utterances. Thus, there is a tacit assumption that children already know quite a lot about grammar before they are able to actually use syntax to say sentences.

This study represents an attempt to explain the emergence of grammar by looking at changes in children's USE of single-word utterances in the period of time before they use syntax in their speech — specifically, by looking at linguistic behavior in relation to the nonlinguistic behavior and context which go along with what children hear and what they say. Children need to evaluate the speech that they hear, to be sure, but they can do so only in relation to certain of their other experiences of the world in order to learn to talk. It will be shown that to characterize children's speech only in terms of the form of their utterances — that is, the fact that they say only one word at a time — is to ignore essential aspects of a complex and changing period of development[2].

The principal conclusions of this study are, first, that children say only one word at a time because of both linguistic and psycho-

---

[2] Although the study of single-word utterances reported here and the recent studies of emerging grammar reported elsewhere have described children's speech, there has never been an intention to imply that how children understand or process the speech that they hear in this same period of time is of lesser importance. To be sure, both kinds of studies contribute to knowledge of what children know about language. However, studies of children's comprehension in the first two years are notoriously difficult in virtually every respect. The study of how children use speech is only relatively less difficult.

logical limitations; but, in particular, they do not know as much about sentences in this period of time as has so often been assumed. Second, what children do know at different points in this period of time, in terms of their cognitive development, appears to influence the linguistic inductions they make about the grammar of their language, so that different children may approach the learning of syntax with different strategies at different points in the single-word utterance period.

The theoretical framework for the study evolved directly from a major result of the psycholinguistic studies of emerging grammar in the last decade. Given the evidence we now have about the conceptual relations that children express in their first sentences[3], it is possible to ask: do younger children express the same or similar conceptual notions with pre-syntax single-word utterances? As will be seen, the distinctions among the kinds of conceptual relations coded in early sentences appear to be related to children's use of single-word utterances before syntax, and also to the potentially different strategies for learning to say two-word utterances.

The report that follows is divided into four major sections. Chapter 2 presents several alternative arguments that have been offered in the literature for explaining the transition from the use of only one word at a time to the use of two-word utterances — which happens, for many children, sometime in the second half of the second year. It will be seen that most theoretical and descriptive accounts depend upon the basic assumption that children's single-word utterances are one-word 'sentences' or 'holophrases'. This assumption, and the implicit claim it presupposes about linguistic knowledge of grammar or structure at this stage, will eventually be refuted (in Chapter 3). An alternative account will be offered that explains children's use of single-word utterances in terms of their developing COGNITIVE capacities. Following this introduction to theories of transition in Chapter 2, there is an account of the

---

[3] Lois Bloom, *Language development*, 1970; I. M. Schlesinger, "Production of utterances and language acquisition", in Dan I. Slobin (ed.), *The ontogenesis of grammar*, 1971; Roger Brown, "*A first language, stage I: Semantic and grammatical relations*", in prep. (See Sec. 2.2.)

conceptual relations encoded in early sentences. Chapter 2 concludes with a discussion of the origin of sentences in terms of
contemporary linguistic theory and notions of 'input' to grammar.

Chapter 3 presents the argument that single-word utterances
before children use syntax in their speech are NOT 'sentences'. In
particular, two major hypotheses that have been offered repeatedly
in the literature to explain the child's limitation to producing only
one word at a time will be refuted. Both hypotheses are based
on the notion of insufficiency: (1) children are not able to say
more than one word at a time because of immature memory, or
physiological inability to actually produce longer utterances, and
(2) children do not combine words because they do not yet know
enough words (insufficient lexicon). Data will be presented to
demonstrate that both of these claims are false; there is evidence
from one child who was able to produce longer ORDERED utterances
five months before she used word order to code semantic relationships, and there is evidence from four children who used many
words to make reference to many persons, objects and relations
before combining such words in ordered relationship.

Chapter 4 describes one child's use of single-word utterances in
terms of the developmental change in both form and function of
words over the twelve-month period during which they were used,
before the emergence of grammar in her speech at approximately
21 months. It will be seen that learning grammar does not depend
in any simple way on the gradual accumulation of words and word
meanings, and the use of one-word utterances is not a single stage
of development, nor merely a developmental 'milestone'.

The last chapter discusses the conceptual notions underlying
single-word utterances, and concludes with a proposed account of
the origin of grammar in terms of two alternative strategies for
learning syntax that explain the transition from one word at a time
to two-word utterances in the speech of different children.

These are the issues that were taken up in this study; the evidence
that will be considered was obtained from two sources. The
principal source of data is a diary record of my daughter, Allison,
begun with the appearance of her first words at nine months and

concluded with the use of sentences at 22 months. This diary record is neither as complete nor as meticulous as that reported, for example, by Werner Leopold[4]. No attempt was made to record every utterance; rather, notes were made and examples of speech events recorded at weekly intervals. These notes were supplemented by four 40-minute video tape records made at intervals in which a substantive change had been observed in Allison's use of speech; the video records were made at ages 16 months, 3 weeks; 19 months, 2 weeks; 20 months, 3 weeks; and 22 months. Transcriptions of these video records that include both the linguistic and nonlinguistic data are included as an Appendix.

The secondary source of data is audio tape records of samples of speech from three children — Eric, Gia and Jane — obtained just previous to their use of sentences. The subsequent emergence of grammar in the language development of Eric and Gia has already been described[5]. The material obtained from Jane has not been reported before. All three children were seen individually, in their homes; two observations of Eric were four and six hours long; Gia was seen for seven hours and Jane for nine hours. Eric and Gia were each 19 months, one week old; Jane was 18 months, two weeks old[6].

The data from Eric, Gia and Jane were obtained towards the end of the single-word utterance period. The early Allison diary notes and, most significantly, the first three video tapes of Allison complement and extend the information obtained from Eric, Gia and Jane in attempting to explain the transition from the use of single-word utterances to the use of syntax in child speech.

---

[4] Werner Leopold, *Speech development of a bilingual child*, 1939-1949. As will be seen, Leopold's diary study of his daughter Hildegard's language development has many echoes in the research reported here. His was, as far as I can tell, the most thorough and the most insightful of the great diary studies. References to the Leopold diary in the remainder of the text that follows refer to Vols. 1 or 3, and will not be documented further, unless direct quotations are presented.

[5] In Lois Bloom, *Language development*, 1970.

[6] There is an extensive description of the procedures used to collect these data in Lois Bloom, *Language development*, 1970, 15-16; 234-240.

SINGLE-WORD UTTERANCES AND GRAMMAR

2.1. EXPLAINING THE TRANSITION TO SYNTAX

There are at least four explanations for the transition from single-word utterances to syntax in early child speech: that children simply hear and remember all possible sentences; that learning syntax depends upon children learning the permitted linguistic contexts of words or the order of words relative to other words in the speech they hear; that children in the single-word utterance period already have knowledge of the basic grammatical or semantic structures of sentences, and single-word utterances are 'sentences'; and, finally, the conclusion of this study — that children learn a language as a linguistic coding of developmentally prior conceptual representations of experience.

The least plausible explanation is that children hear, store, and eventually use and understand sentences paired with appropriate contexts or situations. Children do learn certain fixed expressions that are appropriate to certain specific states of affairs; Leopold called such phenomena "stereotype sentences". Although they may not occur in the speech of all children to the same extent, they have been reported often enough that the question of their relevance to early syntax can be raised. For example, the utterance "have that one", when used by a child repeatedly in a situation in which he wants to have a particular object, is an example of an expression that is produced with specific semantic intent and is appropriate to the situation in which it occurs. Two children from whom I have only anecdotal information used such utterances as "I wanta _____",

"I wanta go _____", "I'm hungry" as their first 'syntactic' utterances. However, the obvious evidence against a model of language development based upon hearing and storing all possible sentences is that children are exposed to only a sample of possible sentences, and the number of possible sentences in natural languages is potentially infinite. Children hear only those sentences spoken in their environment, but they nevertheless come to speak and understand sentences that they have never heard before.

A second explanation for the transition to syntax was suggested by Braine[1]. From evidence obtained through experiments with adults learning artificial languages, and from evidence of the distribution of words in children's early two-word sentences, Braine proposed a theory for learning syntax based on "contextual generalization". In this view, children learn syntax by learning the relative position of words as they occur in the adult sentences to which they are exposed. As will be seen presently, this explanation is only a partial one, at best. The relevance of artificial language learning to children's first language learning is necessarily limited. Artificial languages are meaningless, consisting only of empty formal arrangements of elements. The cooccurrence of items in possible sentences of an artificial language is motivated only by position — the code that is used to formulate such sentences is based only upon the relative distribution or order of 'words'. In contrast, the cooccurrence of words in children's spontaneous sentences is motivated, quite simply, by what they intend to say — by the meaning relationship between the words that occur together.

A third explanation of the emergence of syntax is contained in the view that children's single-word utterances before syntax somehow represent 'sentences'. There is a long tradition in the study of child language that describes children's single-word utterances before syntax as holophrastic or 'one-word sentences'. On the one hand, if the notion of 'sentence' is taken to be a structural specification for the relationship between elements, then one might wonder

---

[1]   Martin D. S. Braine, "On learning the grammatical order of words", *Psychological Review*, 1963. See, also, Kirk Smith and Martin D. S. Braine, "Artificial language learning and language acquisition", in press.

how a child's utterances can be described as sentences when they occur only as isolated elements. On the other hand, Lewis, among others, has observed that "when the child first uses and responds to adult words referentially, he is referring not so much to an object — a thing within the situation — as to the situation as a whole. ... A word that the child speaks ... [is] the means by which he responds to a situation, as an essential part of his total reaction to it."[2] Few would argue Lewis's point. However, whether or not such single-word utterances can or should be structurally represented as 'sentences' is an important question for a theory of the origins of knowledge of grammar.

In the extreme version of this view, single-word utterances are seen as 'intending' or somehow representing sentences, so that subsequent development consists of filling in predictable omissions as the child's memory span, physiological capacity, and knowledge of lexical items and syntactic markers increase with maturation. The evidence usually cited to support the holophrastic account of single words includes: the variations in intonation and stress which accompany such words[3]; the accompanying gestures which can be seen as expansions of meaning[4]; the propositional value of such utterances as they are interpreted by adults in the environment[5]; and the transitive, relational nature of their interpretation[6]. Further, it has often been assumed that children's ability to understand exceeds their speaking ability at every stage of language development[7]. The implication of this claim is that analysis of syntactic structure is somehow involved in such comprehension, so that

[2] M. M. Lewis, *Infant speech, a study of the beginnings of language*, 1951, 159-160.
[3] Paula Menyuk, *Sentences children use*, 1969, 25-29; Eric Lenneberg, *Biological foundations of language*, 1967, 283.
[4] David Ingram, "Transitivity in child language", *Language*, 1971.
[5] Grace de Laguna, *Speech: Its function and development*, 1927; 1963.
[6] David McNeill, *The acquisition of language: The study of developmental psycholinguistics*, 1970; Joshua Smith, "The development and structure of holophrases", 1970; and David Ingram, "Transitivity in child language", 1971.
[7] See, for example, Colin Fraser, Ursula Bellugi and Roger Brown, "Control of grammar in imitation, comprehension and production", *Journal of Verbal Learning and Verbal Behavior*, 1963.

understanding depends on a knowledge of syntax that is not evident from the child's use of single-word utterances.

Thus, variations in prosody, the expanded interpretation by adults that is possible for single-word utterances, and the presumed ability of children to understand more than they say are the principal factors in specifying single-word utterances as holophrases or primitive sentences. The most persuasive argument in favor of this position is that it offers a strong explanation for the transition to syntax. It certainly makes the eventual occurrence of sentences easier to account for if one posits the existence of 'knowledge' of sentences before they actually occur. However, much of the evidence that has been offered to support the view of single-word utterances as holophrastic is conjectural and based on anecdotal reports. There have been no systematic studies of intonation and stress at this stage to determine contrastive status, as Menyuk has pointed out[8], and recent studies of comprehension at this stage and later[9] appear to contradict the view that comprehension generally precedes production. In section 2.3, which follows, two different theories of 'holophrastic' speech will be considered in greater detail.

Whether or not children do have pre-syntax knowledge of grammar may well be unknowable; that is, it is not clear that any amount

---

[8] Paula Menyuk, *Sentences children use*, 1969. Menyuk has since reported a study of the differential use of prosody in single-word utterances (*The acquisition and development of language*, 1971, 61-62). Adult judges were asked to identify different prosodic patterns in children's speech and, not at all surprisingly, there was a high correlation reported for the judges' identification of different, recognizable patterns of intonation and stress. However, the fact that such patterns can be reliably identified is not evidence of their having different CONTRASTIVE status. One would need to determine whether or not different prosody patterns FUNCTION differently, or 'mean' different things — that what children DO with what they say is, alternatively, to ask QUESTIONS or make STATEMENTS. The fact that the different prosodic contours of single-word utterances can be discriminated by adults has long been apparent to even the most casual observer. That such different contours do indeed contrast with one another in their function remains to be demonstrated. (See the discussion of early prosody and syntax which follows in Chapter 3.)

[9] Elizabeth Shipley, Carlota Smith, and Lila Gleitman, "A study in the acquisition of language: Free responses to commands", *Language*, 1969; Charles Fernald, "Children's active and passive knowledge of syntax", 1970.

or kind of evidence can demonstrate convincingly that children know about sentences before they say sentences. Why, then, should one bother to dispute the claim that they do? Essentially, the argument is worth pursuing because one would like to be able to explain why children do not use syntax at this time, why it is they begin to use syntax when they do, and, perhaps most important, one would like to account for what it is they do know at this age — if WHAT they know is not grammar.

An alternative explanation for the emergence of syntax — and the one proposed here — is that children perceive and organize their experience of the world in the first two years in terms of certain conceptual representations that are not linguistic. Sometime during the second year, the child begins to discover aspects of the linguistic code that, in the language of his environment, can represent certain conceptions of experience. It is proposed that before the use of syntax in their speech, children have little if any knowledge of linguistic structure, and that children learn syntax as a mapping or coding of their underlying cognitive representations.

2.2. CONCEPTUAL RELATIONS IN EARLY SENTENCES

The conceptual notions expressed in children's single-word utterances can be analyzed within a framework provided by a description of the conceptual relations that have been identified in the early two-word utterances of older children. That is, knowing the kinds of things children talk about when they first use sentences, it is reasonable to look for similar notions in linguistically earlier data, as evidence of input to learning grammar. In the earlier study of emerging grammar it was shown that certain conceptual notions were expressed over and over again in the speech of three children (Eric, Gia and Kathryn). That is, when the 'meaning' of utterances was inferred from the relation between what the children said and the behavior and context with which their utterances occurred, it was apparent that the semantic intentions represented in these early two-word utterances could be attributed to a relatively small number of consistently recurring underlying conceptual notions or relations[10].

It was possible to identify two different kinds of semantic relationship between words in two-word utterances. In one, there was semantic relationship between words that was relatively independent of the separate meanings of the individual words in the utterance. That is, there were certain recurring structural meanings that (1) occurred with different words and (2) derived from the transitive relationship between the words (as, for example, between actor and action, action and goal, agent and object). Particular words, for example, "Mommy" or "sock", occurred with specific function (that is, agent or object) only relative to each other (or to other words). Such meaning relationships are coded in English by the BASIC GRAMMATICAL RELATIONS (subject-verb-object) of sentences. In the second kind of semantic relationship between words, the relational meaning between the words was dependent upon the meaning of one of the words. That is, there were certain words (such as "more" and "no") that occurred with (1) many different words and (2) consistent semantic function (such as coding the notions 'recurrence' and 'nonexistence').

The large majority of the two-word sentences in the speech of Eric, Gia and Kathryn could be structurally specified in terms of the basic grammatical relations of English sentences. Two nouns in juxtaposition most often specified the relation between subject (either agent of action, or possession, or object located) and predicate object (that is, object of action, or possession, or location of object). Verb-forms occurred with following nouns in direct object relation, and in predicate relation with preceding agent-actor

[10] Lois Bloom, *Language development*, 1970. The terms SEMANTIC and CONCEPTUAL are used here with the intention of distinguishing between the meanings of particular words or the meaning relations between words (SEMANTICS), and the underlying cognitive structures (CONCEPTS or thoughts) that represent the relations among persons, objects and events in the world. A grammar is seen here as a system of rules for specifying semantic-syntactic relationships among words in sentences. Grammar, and the structures of syntax and semantics, represent LINGUISTIC knowledge. The COGNITIVE underpinnings of language are the organization and representation of perceived reality.

nouns. All such grammatical relations were not present to the same extent from the beginning, and they did not appear in the speech of the three children in the same developmental sequence in the period from 19 to 23 months. Eric used utterances with action verb and object before he began to produce subject-verb utterances. Gia used two nouns together before she used verb forms in relation to either subject or object nouns. Kathryn, who was first seen at a somewhat later point in linguistic development than either Eric or Gia, produced two-word utterances with the grammatical relations subject–object, verb–object, and subject–verb.

The meaning of the relationship between words in other sentences could not be described in terms of basic grammatical relations. The relational meaning in such sentences derived from the meaning of one of the two words. Certain words such as "no", "no more", "more" and "this" occurred in contexts with noun forms (for example, "no sock", "no more noise", "more raisin", "this book") and verb forms (for example, "no fit", "more read", "this cleaning"). These words occurred frequently, with a large number of different forms. They also occurred as single-word utterances. However, the most important aspect of their occurrence in the children's speech was the fact that they each occurred in situations that shared features of context and behavior. Their occurrence was motivated by what the children were talking about, that is, by what the children meant by what they said.

Utterances with "no", "no more", and, marginally, "all gone" occurred in situations in which the object (or action) specified did not exist (or did not occur), although there was some reason for expectation of its existence (or occurrence). Kathryn said "no pocket" when she could not find a pocket in her mother's skirt; Kathryn said "no fit" when one block did not fit into another; Eric said "no more noise" when the vacuum cleaner stopped. Thus, utterances with "no" in Kathryn's and Gia's speech or "no more" in Eric's speech were used by the children to comment on the NONEXISTENCE of objects (or non-occurrence of events)[11].

---

[11]   Actually, the notion of NONEXISTENCE as described in Lois Bloom, *Language development*, 1970, can be differentiated into narrower conceptual categories

"More" (or "'nother") was among the most frequent words used by the children and did not occur as a comparative term. Rather, all of the instances of "more" (as a single-word utterance or in syntactic combination) commented on or requested the RECURRENCE or another instance of the referent, after previous occurrence. Kathryn said "more raisin" when she wanted raisins again, "more block" when she took another block from a box; Gia said "more read" when she picked up another book to be read to her.

The EXISTENCE of a referent in the context was commented on most simply by the use of "ə" (for example, "ə raisin", "ə fit") or, in Kathryn's speech, with the demonstrative pronouns "this" or "that" (which were not contrastive).

Thus, in addition to sentences in which conceptual relations between persons, objects, and events were coded by the BASIC GRAMMATICAL RELATIONS subject-object, verb-object, subject-verb, there were other sentences in which different conceptual notions — existence, nonexistence, and recurrence — were coded by the FUNCTIONAL RELATIONS between words. The meaning of such sentences derived from the inherently relational meaning of the function forms, for example, "more", "no", and "this". It is important to point out that the distinction between the two kinds of semantic relations — grammatical relations and functional relations — in these early sentences was not based on distributional evidence. Utterances with "ə", "no", "no more", "this", and "more" were superficially 'pivotal'[12] — the function forms were small in number, they occurred frequently, in fixed position, with a large number of different, substantive, forms. However, certain of the substantive forms in sentences with the basic grammatical relations had the same distribution — in particular "Mommy", reference to self ("Baby", "Kathryn", "Gia"), "raisin", and "fit". These words also

---

(for example, DISAPPEARANCE and CESSATION) as reported in the discussion of the use of 'negative' single-words which follows in Chapter 4.

[12] As described originally by Martin D. S. Braine, "The ontogeny of English phrase structure", 1963. See Lois Bloom, "Why not pivot grammar?", *Journal of Speech and Hearing Disorders*, 1971, for a critique of the adequacy of the 'pivot grammar' account for describing early sentences.

occurred frequently, in fixed position, with a large number of different words, and, by distributional criteria alone could also be described as 'pivotal'. The distinction between the two kinds of semantic relations between words in these early sentences was determined by the coordination of inferred semantic intent with underlying structural relationship.

Certain conceptual relations which might have been expected to be expressed in children's early sentences did not occur. The occurrence of attributive or predicate adjectives was rare, with no reference to relative size, color, or quantity; there was no instance of the dative (indirect object); there was no expression of identity ("Mommy lady") or disjunction (either-or relationship). Rather, the children talked about the existence, nonexistence, and recurrence of objects and events, the location of objects, the possessive relation between persons and objects, and relations between an action and the agent OR goal (locative or direct object) of the action. Thus, the children were selective in what they chose to talk about, and it was not the case that their utterances were merely the linguistic reflections of the many possible interactions among persons, objects and events in the environment. Instead, it appeared that the children's utterances manifested specific linguistic capacities with the ability to represent or code only a limited number of conceptual distinctions.

2.2.1. *Additional Evidence*

The account of underlying conceptual relations in the early sentences of three children — Kathryn, Eric, and Gia — would have greater validity for use as a framework for the analysis of single-word utterances before syntax if one could predict some degree of generality of these results among other children. Just this kind of support for the above account can be found in several recent reports[13].

[13] I. M. Schlesinger, "Production of utterances and language acquisition", 1971; Roger Brown, "*A first language*", in prep.; and Melissa Bowerman, "Learning to talk: A cross-linguistic study of early syntactic development, with special reference to Finnish", 1970.

Schlesinger, in an analysis of the child speech data available in the literature before 1968, proposed a model for a semantic input to early grammar that was based on the relations between forms. He proposed a similar distinction as above between relational pairs on the one hand, including the relations between agent, action and direct object, modifier and head (specifying both attributive and possessive forms and "more" as 'modifier') and subject and locative; and different utterances which were described as 'operations' on the other hand. The 'operations' expressed negation and ostension (using an 'introducer' such as "this", "that", "here", "there") and were not considered relational: "negation does not hold between two elements, but operates on one element".

Bowerman studied the speech of one American child and two Finnish-speaking children. She found evidence of similar semantic relations between words in early two-word utterances in both languages and concluded that such semantic relationship between words was the source of early structure in child speech. Brown found similar evidence of the above semantic-conceptual relations in his analysis of the speech of his three American subjects as well as the data in Finnish, Russian, and Chinese. He argued for the universality of such semantic relations in early syntactic child speech. Table 1 presents the semantic categorization of early sentences proposed by Bloom, Schlesinger, and Brown. Although this kind of information was obtained from conclusions reached about the speech of less than twenty children, there appears to be enough evidence to conclude that the conceptual relations that are represented are not idiosyncratic[14].

2.3. THE ORIGIN OF SENTENCES AND LINGUISTIC THEORY

The underlying organization of early sentences in terms of the conceptual relations that have been described can be represented in

[14] Although all such relations do not appear to be represented to the same extent in the speech of different children, and some may not be represented at all, all such conceptual notions as have been identified appear to form a limited

TABLE 1

Semantic Categorization of Two-Word Sentences

Bloom[a]	Schlesinger[b]	Brown[c]
A. *Functional Relations*	A. *Operations*	A. *Operators of Reference*
1. Existence	1. Negation	1. Nomination
2. Nonexistence	2. Ostension	2. Recurrence
3. Recurrence		3. Nonexistence
B. *Grammatical Relations*	B. *Relations*	B. *Semantic Relations*
4. Agent, Action, Object	3. Agent, Action, Object	4. Agent, Action, Object
5. Possessive	4. Modifier and Head (includes attributive and possessive)	5. Affected Person, State, Object
6. Attributive		6. Locative
7. Locative	5. Locative	7. Possessive and Attributive
	6. Dative (one instance)	8. Demonstrative
		9. Dative

[a]   Lois Bloom, *Language development*, 1970; "Why not pivot grammar?", 1971.
[b]   I. M. Schlesinger, "Production of utterances and language acquisition", 1971.
[c]   Roger Brown, *A first language*, in prep.

two alternative ways. If grammar is viewed as a semantically based construct, then the underlying conceptual relations can be seen as providing the semantic input to the syntactic component of the grammar. In this view, the notions that have been described — the relation between the AGENT of an action and the OBJECT of that action, for example — are 'semantic primitives' which are encoded by syntax. This was essentially the model for early child grammar proposed by Schlesinger: that children learn notions of agent, action, object as concepts which are realized or mapped onto the early syntactic utterances. Thus, the syntactic component of a grammar for child language would function to provide the means whereby such semantic information is realized in sentences[15].

---

set. That is, children may or may not have learned to talk about one or another such aspect of experience, but it does not appear to be the case that they do code different notions or relations instead.

[15]   Schlesinger's account is within the framework of a 'generative semantics'

Alternatively, one might argue that the essentially relational nature of the notions expressed in early sentences depends upon an underlying syntactic basis — that the conceptual notions are not more nor less than the semantic interpretation of basic syntactic information. In this view the existence of such semantic notions (or such evidence of conceptual relations) in sentences depends upon (as interpretations of) the syntax of the sentence. This is the framework on which the theory of child grammar proposed by McNeill is based[16]. In McNeill's view, such relational notions that exist in early sentences exist only by virtue of the basic subject-predicate relation in syntactic structure. Thus, the existence of any such 'grammatical relations' in child speech (whether realized as a single-word or multi-word utterance) is taken as evidence of the developmentally prior existence of the structural notion of 'sentence'. However rudimentary or primitive the notion of 'sentence' may be for the child, it is nonetheless a structural specification for syntactic relationship.

More recently, Chomsky has argued that the differences between the two versions of deep structure — in particular, the levels and function of semantic and syntactic representation in the deep structure of sentences — are less real than would appear from the extent of the argument. He concluded that the 1965 'standard' theory needs revision with respect to the role of semantics in surface structure, but he rejected a semantically based deep structure on the grounds that it does not change the essential nature of the base component in any important way and that, indeed, there are certain problems that it will not solve as well as will the 'standard' theory[17].

---

such as has been proposed by Charles Fillmore, "The case for case", in Emmon Bach and Robert T. Harms (eds.), *Universals in linguistic theory*, 1968, and George Lakoff, "Instrumental adverbs and the concept of deep structure", *Foundations of language*, 1968.

[16] David McNeill, *The acquisition of language*, 1970. McNeill's theories derive from the essentially 'interpretive' semantic grammar component in the linguistic theory of Noam Chomsky, *Aspects of the theory of syntax*, 1965, and Jerrold Katz and Paul Postal, *An integrated theory of linguistic descriptions*, 1964.

[17] Noam Chomsky, "Deep structure, surface structure and semantic interpretation", in Danny Steinberg and Leon A. Jakobovits (eds.), *Semantics: An inter-disciplinary reader in philosophy, linguistics and psychology*, 1971.

The theoretical argument about the role of semantics in grammar is based on attempts to account for the correct derivations of particular sentences in some abstract sense. It is less concerned with the nature of speakers and the origins of sentences as mental operations. There is a necessary distinction between the grammar that is proposed as a linguistic hypothesis for the specification of sentences that are possible in the language on the one hand, and the behavioral and cognitive functions underlying sentences that are spoken and understood on the other. This distinction was made by Chomsky, Fodor and Garrett, and is discussed at length in Watt[18]. However, the distinction has been blurred in actuality more often than not. There has been a strong inclination to view the theory of generative grammar as at least potentially isomorphic with operations of the mind in speaking and understanding sentences. In this respect, the form of any linguistic theory can be mistakenly seen as axiomatic for a theory of language development.

Two recent views of the origins of grammar in pre-syntax behavior have been developed in just this way from the two alternative theories: 'generative' and 'interpretive' semantics. Ingram[19] used the theory of grammar that views syntax as following from a semantic basis to account for the semantically transitive (relational) nature of certain single-word utterances. For example, the child's use of "up" with reflexive OBJECT (self) and speaker (self) as AGENT when she has gotten up, is contrasted with "up" with speaker as OBJECT (self, non-reflexive) and hearer as AGENT when she wants to be picked up (Ingram's examples are from Leopold's diary record). The two occurrences of "up" were distinguished by Ingram according to the features attributed to AGENT and OBJECT in the respective underlying representations of the word "up".

There were three additional, contrasting uses of "up" reported by

[18]   Noam Chomsky, *Aspects of the theory of syntax*, 1965, 9; Noam Chomsky, *Language and mind*, 1968, 23; Jerry A. Fodor and Merrill Garrett, "Some reflections on competence and performance", in John Lyons and Roger Wales (eds.), *Psycholinguistics papers*, 1966, 135-154; William C. Watt, "On two hypotheses concerning psycholinguistics", in John R. Hayes (ed.), *Cognition and the development of language*, 1970, 137-220.

[19]   David Ingram, "Transitivity in child language", 1971.

Leopold — one in which something inanimate (a periodical) was put up on a mantel, one a report about Mama having gotten up (where "[-speaker; -hearer] is the reflexive agent", and, presumably, the object as well), and the direction to (get) "up" with the hearer as AGENT and reflexive OBJECT. There was good evidence to indicate that Leopold's daughter knew the notion of 'upness' in relation to objects and people, including herself. However, evidence that would support the contention that her knowledge of the meaning of the word took the form of different underlying relationships between AGENTS and OBJECTS which were potentially animate, human and reflexive is not given. Such an account of single-word utterances in terms of semantically based grammatical relations may be a stronger linguistic account than is necessary to explain the occurrence of "up". The meaning of the word depends upon antecedent phenomena, to be sure. But the child's cognizance of such phenomena in relation to the word "up" is a function of the underlying conceptual notion itself. No other formal specification is justified (or even necessary). There is, quite simply, the fact that "up" depends for its meaning on its transitive relation to some aspect of the situation, which may be only partially defined by the child thus far, and not represented at all in the conceptions that underlie the use of "up". This discussion of the conceptual representations of words such as "up" will be resumed subsequently in Chapter 5.

It is McNeill's contention that "virtually everything that occurs in language acquisition depends on PRIOR knowledge of the basic aspects of sentence structure. The concept of a sentence may be part of man's innate mental capacity. ... The facts of language could not be as they are unless the concept of a sentence is available to children at the start of their learning." McNeill goes on to cite the theory of Grace de Laguna, who described children's single-word utterances as predications or propositional comments which "function as complete rudimentary sentences". McNeill reports a "constant emergence of new grammatical relations, even though no utterance is ever longer than one word". "Thus, very young children develop a concept of a sentence as a set of grammatical relations before they develop a concept of how these relations are expressed." The subsequent development of grammar is certainly easier to explain than would be the case if the child did not already know so much about sentences. And, indeed, McNeill reports that the combination of words "is not the appearance of grammar but the appearance of patterned speech to express grammar"[20].

McNeill's theory then is that the relational nature of children's utterances results from the interpretation of an underlying structural basis. He asserts that children do not merely 'name' or 'label' objects, people, and events in their environment — they propositionalize, and they could not possibly engage in such behavior unless they were somehow equipped with a linguistic MECHANISM for doing so.

McNeill's account raises many more questions than it answers about the nature of language development. It attributes to the child certain capabilities for learning at an even earlier age than would otherwise be expected in a search for the origins of grammar. How is it possible for the child, in the first 18 months of life — when he has just about come to terms with such basic facts about his environment as the permanence of objects — to 'know' so much about the abstract nature of a linguistic code? To be sure, McNeill himself appears to recognize the difficulties in the child's task and so posits the "prior" and "innate" existence of much linguistic information. But, again, the 'answer' leads to far more fundamental questions about the nature of innate endowment in general, and the structure and function of an innate linguistic endowment in particular.

The question of a semantic basis versus a syntactic basis in the underlying specification of sentences is an important issue in attempting to explain the emergence of grammar only to the extent that a theory of linguistics, as a theory of language, can somehow account for the cognitive and behavioral aspects as well as formal aspects of language. Semantic and syntactic categories are necessarily linguistic categories, determined by formal criteria of arrangement and relationship. The distinctions between the 'subject-of-the-

---

[20]   David McNeill, *The acquisition of language*, 1970, 2, 22-23, 25.

predicate' and the 'agent-of-the-action' or the 'object-of-the-verb' and the 'object-of-the-action' are distinctions among domains of linguistic categories. The important distinction for the child's learning language is more likely between LINGUISTIC categories — categories that are dependent on semantic and syntactic specification of relationship — on the one hand, and COGNITIVE categories on the other hand, which are dependent on the mental representation of experience. If the child learns language as a linguistic coding of certain cognitive representations of his experience as it is proposed here, then it is necessary to question the use of the notion of a 'sentence' as 'input' for the child's learning grammar. It will be argued, in the discussion that follows, that the emergence of grammar towards the end of the second year derives from and depends upon an underlying COGNITIVE basis. In short, children using single-word utterances know little if anything about sentences, but they have begun to know considerably more about the world of objects, events, and relations.

3

SINGLE-WORD UTTERANCES ARE NOT SENTENCES

The nature of the words that occur in the single-word utterance period, the ways in which certain of the words appear to be used, and what appears to many observers to be the child's comprehension of complex speech, have led to the claim that children have knowledge of linguistic structure before they use it. Several different arguments will be presented to dispute this claim that children have knowledge of 'sentences' before they are able to actually use sentences in their speech. To begin with, the only direct evidence that children do not know about grammar before they use sentences, is the simple fact that they do not ordinarily SAY sentences or phrases. Except for instances that are too occasional to be considered important as evidence of underlying productivity, young children say only one word at a time in the first half of the second year. However, there is other evidence, that is necessarily indirect, to counter the claim that single-word utterances are sentences.

Two major phenomena will be described and discussed: (1) the occurrence of utterances longer than one word that do not contain more than one word, and (2) the occurrence of single words in succession that are not conjoined, within the bounds of a single speech event, that is, single-word utterances that share topic and context. Further, (3) the supposed comprehension of more complex speech than is produced, and (4) the use of different prosody contours during the time when children use single-word utterances will be discussed, and alternative views of both these phenomena will be suggested.

3.1. /wídə/: THE ARCHETYPAL PIVOT

It is generally suggested, either tacitly or otherwise, that part of the explanation for the child's not using syntax lies in the immaturity of memory and physiological capacity to sustain a longer utterance. But children often produce extended strings of sounds that are unintelligible, but that appear to reproduce or mimic adult patterns of sentence intonation. This kind of expressive vocalization, 'jargon', or 'mature babbling' is reported often in the literature and by parents and appears to represent the child's attempt to imitate the acoustic, superficial aspects of adult speech. Clearly, the child can actually utter a sequence of connected sounds that is considerably longer than a single word.

Eric used such expressive vocalization to a greater extent than the other children, but it could not be analyzed into constituent parts[1]. It was concluded that, although he could produce extended vocalization that was phonetically varied, the individual sounds were not juxtaposed in any systematic way, that is, they were not phonemically structured in relation to one another. Thus, strings of sounds were produced but they were not word-like in terms of phonetic juncture or relationship. Memory and physiological support, then, might well be two features that constrain the length and complexity of early intelligible utterances. It could be that the child cannot 'remember' the consistent and relevant phonetic connections, or physically produce the more complex phonemic sequences that two-word forms would involve. However, there was a phenomenon recorded in Allison's speech during a three-week period at age 16 months which strongly indicated that the factors of immature memory or physiological capacity for speech were not the relevant factors operating in restricting her to using only word at a time.

At 16 months, one week, the following speech event occurred: Allison looked at her father sitting across the dining table from her, reading the newspaper, and she commented "Dada wídə". I

---

[1] Described in Lois Bloom, *Language development*, 1970, 102-103.

responded, "Yes, Daddy's reading the newspaper" and I made a note of the utterance as "Dada read(ing)". The next day, the following occurred: Allison and I had waited with Mimi (her babysitter) for the elevator; as Mimi entered the elevator to leave, Allison commented "Mimi wídə̀". I recorded the utterance as "Mimi elevator". Within several days it became quite clear that neither of these utterances represented what I had interpreted and recorded them to be. For a period of three weeks, the form "wídə̀" occurred more often than any other word (including person names); it rarely occurred in isolation; and it dropped from use just as suddenly as it had appeared. There were two features that characterized Allison's use of "wídə̀" — the lack of any identifiable consistent referent and the remarkable consistency in its ordered occurrence in juxtaposition with other words in apparent 'syntactic' combinations.

What was "wídə̀"? As with the two first examples recorded and just described, there did not appear to be any features of context or behavior that were shared by the speech events in which "wídə̀" occurred. Its appearance in Allison's speech was noticed by all who knew her and on occasion strangers who heard her asked the same question: "What is 'wídə̀'?" Its use was discussed in the seminar referred to earlier, with friends and family at home, and with large numbers of students and colleagues who have since seen the video tape made at 16, 3 on which Allison's use of "wídə̀" is amply documented. (See the Appendix for the complete transcription of the video tape at 16, 3.)

A number of guesses have been made, and among the interpretations offered there are two recurring observations of "wídə̀": it occurred often in action events, as Allison either did something, or something happened; and it also occurred in situations where Allison wanted to have or to do something. But, it was also the case that much of what Allison otherwise said occurred in action events or when she wanted to do or to have something. Pending an insight that might indicate otherwise, it has been concluded that "wídə̀" apparently referred to anything and everything, and thus it 'meant' nothing. But its distribution in Allison's speech not only heightened the mystery of its occurrence, but also made it clear that if Allison knew anything about structural notions of grammatical relationship, her not using sentences was not attributable to memory or motor immaturity.

In its distribution in Allison's speech, "wídə" was the perfect PIVOT, as that category of words in child speech was described first by Braine and then by McNeill[2]: it occurred in fixed position, with a number of different words, and it almost never occurred alone. The video tape recording provided clear evidence of its distribution so that description could be made with some confidence. In the course of the 40-minute sample there was a total of 335 intelligible utterances[3], 67 of which included "wídə", and "wídə" occurred as a single word only twice. Seventy-eight of the total number of utterances were longer than a single word, and 65 of these utterances were utterances with "wídə". Following are all of these 'syntactic' utterances with "wídə" and the speech events in which they occurred:[4]

> wídə [77]
> ə wídə [3, 6, 15 (2), 17, 19, 23, 25, 31 (4), 32 (4), 33 (2), 35,
>   38, 50, 56 (3), 57, 58, 61, 67 (2), 81, 83]
> no wídə [37, 53, 56, 59, 77]
> no no wídə [53]
> uh uh no no wídə [37]
> Mama wídə [3, 31 (2), 56 (2)]
> Dada wídə [3, 39]
> uh oh wídə [17, 29, 35 (2), 45, 54 (2), 66]

[2]   Martin D. S. Braine, "The ontogeny of English phrase structure", 1963; David McNeill, "Developmental psycholinguistics", 1966.
[3]   Immediate repetitions were not counted; there were no imitated utterances.
[4]   The transcription of the video tape recorded at 16,3 in the Appendix includes all of these occurrences of "wídə", so that the accompanying behavior and context can be evaluated there. It can be seen that "ə wídə" occurred 31 times, while "wídə" alone occurred only twice. However, "wídə" is presented as the canonical form because it occurred most often without "ə" when juxtaposed with different words. Numbers here in brackets are the event numbers in the transcription; numbers in parentheses refer to the frequency of occurrence within the event.

uh ə wídə [30]
more wídə [30 (2), 56]
more ə wídə [27]
Mama more wídə [21]
Mama ma ə wídə [56]
Mama ma ma ə wídə [56]
oh oh wídə [67]
more ə wí Dada [71]
ə wídə ə wídə [56]
ə wídə pig [67]

Except for the last utterance, "ə wídə pig", and the instance of "ə wídə ə wídə", "wídə" occurred always in final position. It occurred most often after /ə/, and "ə wídə" occurred as a constituent in a longer utterance five times. "More wídə" also occurred as a constituent in a longer utterance. However, it was most significant that, although a total of 30 different words were used in the 335 intelligible utterances that were recorded, "wídə" occurred only with a small number of different words: "uh oh", "more", "no", "Mama", "Dada", and "pig". Seven words occurred 19 times or more in the corpus: "there", "up", "more", "no", "down", "gone", and "baby"; but "wídə" occurred in juxtaposition with only two of these: "more" and "no".

The virtually invariable order of "wídə" relative to the words with which it was combined is of considerable interest. Whether or not "wídə" did 'mean' something for Allison, she was consistent in always placing it AFTER other words in juxtaposition. Thus, she appeared to have learned something about relative position of words in general in English sentences. It was also the case, however, that the words that were combined with "wídə" ("Mama", "Dada", "Baby", "more", "uh oh", "no") were ordered relative to "wídə". Thus, Allison apparently knew something about word order in English sentences in general, but she also appeared to have hypothesized something about likely positions of particular words (for example, person names, "more", and "no") relative to "wídə".

The use of "wídə" in the video tape sample corresponded very closely to its use generally. It occurred in linguistic contexts most often after "ə", and such otherwise frequently used words as "Dada", "Mimi", "Mama", "no", and "more". There were several recorded instances of "Mama Dada wídə" and occasional instances with "car", "plane", and a very few other words. But, there were many more frequently used words with which it never occurred in the course of the three-week period — for example, "gone", "up", "down", and "there". It was always in final position and it rarely occurred alone. Acoustically, there was little difficulty in determining utterance boundaries of the juxtaposed words. There was no intervening pause between 'words', stress was unequal, and there was terminal contour after "wídə".

However, there was no immediately obvious referent for "wídə" — there was no consistency in the features of behavior and context that also occurred. That is not to say that the form had no meaning for Allison; but the nature of its meaning for her could not be determined. It was concluded that the form had no identifiable element of experience, content, or meaning that would distinguish it as a LINGUISTIC fact[5]. Could its use then be described as 'syntactic'? Its distribution in the corpus was nothing if not systematic — it was clearly patterned behavior. But syntax is the arrangement

[5] As per Edward Sapir, *Language*, 1921, 10. In any one of the speech events with "wídə" in the transcript of 16,3, it is possible to identify one or another semantic intent with Allison's behavior. It is certainly not difficult to know what she was talking about and what she wanted in virtually all of these situations. My quizzical "What?" in many of these events was an attempt to have Allison expand or extend her utterances; I knew what she wanted even though I did not understand what she was saying. However, even though one or another 'meaning' can be attributed to "wídə" in one or another of the events at 16,3, when all of these events are taken together, it appears that there is no 'meaning' for "wídə" that is not also intended by some other utterance or gesture (or even by several utterances or gestures taken together).
I am not aware of any report in the literature of similar behavior in other children, but that is not surprising. The "wídə" phenomenon occurred, and it was possible to 'capture' it on video tape, and to study it in considerable detail over a long period of time. Such an occurrence in the speech of other children may well go unnoticed or be considered 'jargon' or 'baby talk'; it flowed along as part of Allison's expressive vocalization. The significance of the "wídə" phenomenon for a theory of early language development became apparent long after "widə" had disappeared.

of words in an utterance relative to each other — an arrangement of words that is determined by the relationship among them. There was no evidence for determining what the relationship might be in utterances with "wídə". It was concluded that "wídə" was an empty pivot. Its occurrence probably indicated that Allison had an awareness of certain superficial facts of speech such as relative word order (of a few forms). More important, however, was the demonstration it provided of the fact that Allison, at 16 months, was not limited to single-word utterances by an immaturity of motor speech production or memory. She could produce two or more clearly discriminable elements in juxtaposition, and remember a consistent order relation between them.

Thus, the Immaturity Hypothesis, offered (at least tacitly) in the literature to account for the limitation to only one word at a time, appears to be improbable. In using "wídə" in juxtaposition with other words, Allison demonstrated that (1) she could 'remember' the permitted positions of different forms relative to one another, and (2) she could say two 'words' together. However she did not use word order to code semantic relationship between word forms. 'Knowing' something about word order was simply not enough. It appeared that the emergence of grammar (the child's early use of relative position or word order to code meaning relations) was not dependent only upon learning the permitted relative position of particular words. Allison presented evidence of knowing something about word order, but she did not go on, at that point, to begin to use sentences. After three weeks, at age 17 months, "wídə" disappeared completely and never occurred again. Allison did not go on to use phrase structure or express semantic relationships in her speech as had been expected. In the video tape corpus at 19,2 — three months later — there were only four utterances longer than a single word, with 316 single-word utterances, and 62 different words. At 16 months, 3 weeks, there had been 78 utterances longer than a single word (including 65 with "wídə"), 272 single-word utterances, and 30 different words.

Beginning at 17 months, there was a marked increase in the number of different lexical items in Allison's speech, and many utterances occurred with no other apparent function than to 'name' or comment on the existence of an object as Allison either looked at it, picked it up, touched it, or pointed to it. Towards the end of that month, shortly before she was 18 months old, there was a substantial increase in the use of successive single-word utterances within the bounds of a single speech event — sequences of two or three words that were not syntactic combinations.

3.2. SUCCESSIVE SINGLE-WORD UTTERANCES

Single-word utterances can most often be interpreted by an adult in relation to particular aspects of the topic and context of speech events. Thus, an utterance occurs as a constituent in a larger construct, the EVENT, which consists of such factors as topic (what is talked about or referred to) and context (which includes speaker and hearer as well as objects, actions, and relations). In child speech events, factors which identify TOPICS are almost always present in CONTEXT. Children talk about what they see and what they do (in what has been called the 'here and now'), in a way that would be most strange for an adult. The redundancy between what a child says and the context and behavior which go along with what he says allows one to identify what it is he is talking about more often than not. Events with separate single-word utterances, then, are distinguishable from one another by shifts in the topic and context with which they occur. However, when more than one utterance occurs without a shift in topic, there is reason to attribute a relationship between them and, indeed, to perceive them as 'successive'.

Throughout the first half of the second year, single-words occurred in speech events that, for the most part, included only a single utterance that was often repeated several times. Allison climbed on a chair and said "up" OR "chair"; she picked up a cookie after having eaten one, and said "more" OR "cookie"; she watched a plane disappear overhead and said "away"; etc. However, there were occasional instances in which she used two words in juxtaposition, as in the examples with "more" in the first video sample at

16,3, in Table 2. There were also instances in which two different single-word utterances were used in the same speech event, and this latter behavior — the use of successive single-word utterances — came to predominate in Allison's speech in the beginning of the second half of her second year. Two words were only rarely joined in apparent syntactic combination at this time. This same phenomenon was observed in the speech of Jane at 18,2 and Eric and Gia at 19,1, before the productive use of syntax (examples below are from the 1970 syntax study)[6]:

(1) Gia at 19,1:

(Gia picking up her mother's slipper)   Mommy/ Mommy/
  What is that?

                                    slipper/
  Slipper.

                                    Mommy/

(2) Gia at 19,1:

(Gia looking at a picture of a boy in a toy car)

                                    go/
  Car.

                                    car/ ride/

(3) Eric at 19,1:

(Eric looking out the window at street below; cars going by; children and adults walking)

                                    car/ see/
  See.

                                    car/
  Car.

                                    boy/

---

[6] Lois Bloom, *Language development*, 1970, 11. In the reported examples of speech events in the text, and in the Appendix, a slash "/" indicates utterance boundary. See Section 1 in the Appendix for a description of the notational convention used for reporting speech events.

Most often, only two or three words occurred in succession, but there were exceptions:

(4) Allison at 18,2:
(Daddy had 'cut' a piece of peach that was
in the bowl of a spoon, with a knife. Alli-
son ate both pieces, then picked up an-
other piece of peach and held it out to
Daddy)   peach/ Daddy/
(Allison picking up the spoon)   spoon/
(Allison giving peach and spoon to Daddy) Daddy/ peach/
                                                   cut/

(5) Allison at 19 months:
(Allison took a pot from the shelf in the
stove and 'stirred' with her hand)   cook/ baby/
    Is the baby cooking?

                                                   pot/ meat/

The prosodic pattern that distinguished such words as these said in succession, as single-word utterances, was unmistakable. Each word occurred with terminal falling pitch contour, and relatively equal stress, and there was a variable but distinct pause between them, so that utterance boundaries were clearly marked. This was in contrast to utterances with "wídә" at 16 months and the occasional examples of two words in juxtaposition. Allison had begun to say two words in juxtaposition at about age 14 months. One or two examples occurred several times each week, and generally included either "more", "away", "stop", or "uh oh" as one of the two constituents. In addition to the longer utterances with "wídә", there were six longer utterances with "more" that were recorded in the video tape sample at 16,3 (see Table 2). However, it is impor- tant to emphasize that in those utterances there was no intervening pause between the words, and utterance boundary was easily placed after the second word, or after "wídә". In short, the early and

TABLE 2

Two or More Words in Juxtaposition, Except "widə"
Allison at 16 months, 3 weeks

10. (A sits down)[a]	uh oh down
22. (A reaching for cookie bag)	more cookie
25. (A reaches in bag)	more cookie
32. (A pulling doll in truck)	ə widə/ baby/ ə baby/ ə widə/ up
42. (A putting man in car)	car away
43. (A getting up, sees doll on floor, walking to doll)	more baby
45. (A picking up doll by the hand)	there mama
74. (A reaching toward cow)	[ə key] = ə cow
75. (A putting cow on table)	more cow
76. (A walks back to chair; picking up pig and putting it on table)	more cow
80. (A turning to sit down on chair)	ə down/ chair/ sit
82. (A looking at pig standing on chair)	uh oh there
84. (A getting other animals from table)	more pig

[a] The numbers of the examples are the numbers of the events in which they occurred, in the transcription in the Appendix.

occasional two-word utterances as well as utterances with "widə" occurred with apparent 'sentence' contour. However, successive single-word utterances at a later time were perceived as separate utterances, because of relatively equal stress, with intervening pause and falling pitch.

There were at least two possible explanations of the occurrence of successive single-word utterances: first, that such speech was merely naming behavior, or, alternatively, that the single words said in succession were somehow related to one another. To begin with, it is possible that Allison, Gia, Jane, and Eric were merely naming or labeling different aspects of the situation. Allison used more words than she had used in previous months, and if we can assume the same was true for Eric, Jane, and Gia, then all four children were able to 'name' more objects, persons, and events in particular contexts. Gia was able to say both "Mommy" and "slipper", whereas earlier she knew fewer words and might have been limited to either "Mommy" or "slipper" in a similar situation. This is perhaps the easiest conclusion to draw — that the child sees Mommy and says "Mommy", sees the slipper and says "slipper". There were examples of successive single-word utterances that appeared to occur in just this way, for example:

(6) (Allison looking at man waiting in
    airport, sitting, with coat and suitcase) man/ chair/ coat/
                                                      suitcase/

However, there were several reasons for concluding that, in most instances, successive single-word utterances were something more than series of words attached to perceived objects. If the children were simply naming aspects of events, then we might expect successive 'naming' to occur as a simple result of knowing more words. It is reasonable, then, to expect the same behavior of most children as vocabularies increase; the more words that a child knows, the more things he would be able to 'name' in a particular event. However, the four children did not produce successive single-word utterances to the same extent. Table 3 presents the number of different words in the samples of speech from Jane at 18,2; Eric both at 19,1 and 20,3; Gia at 19,1; and Allison, for three samples. The samples of speech are not directly comparable;, they differ in duration and size, so that only the grossest comparison among the children is possible. Moreover, we know that Allison, Eric, and Gia were about to use syntax (each at 20-22 months), and we have a record of the form and function of their subsequent syntactic utterances. We do not have a record of Jane's eventual use of syntax, and, therefore, cannot determine the extent of her linguistic maturity at 18,2. If the occurrence of successive single-word utterances merely reflected the child's expanding vocabulary, then one might expect children to use the increased capacity to name in similar ways, but this was not the case. Jane used a greater number

TABLE 3

Total Number of Different Words Used

Child	Age (months, weeks)	Duration of Sample (hours)	Total No. of Utterances	Total No. Different Words
Gia	19,1	7.0	1,015	143
Eric I	19,1	4.0	207	68
Eric II	20,2	6.0	490	108
Jane	18	9.0	860	201
Allison I	16,3	.7	264 (330)[a]	29 (30)[a]
Allison II	19,2	.7	319	61
Allison III	20,3	.7	378	103

[a] Note — Numbers in parentheses include utterances with "wídə".

of different words than the other children, with a lower proportion of successive utterances[7].

Further, not all of the words in succession were 'names' for objects in the context. In (1) "Mommy/slipper" above, Mommy was not there. Such forms as "see", "cut", and "cook" occurred, as well as such words as "up", "more", and "away" — none of which were lexical, substantive forms that 'name' objects. It was probably not the case that successive words simply identified or named objects. Two further observations tended to support this conclusion. First, single-word utterances that were successive because they occurred within the bounds of a single speech event were often interrupted by an utterance from someone else, as in the examples above. In certain instances, utterances in the sequence occurred after a question from someone else, as "slipper" in (1), and "pot/

[7] It should be pointed out that almost half of Jane's utterances were direct or partial imitations of utterances said by someone else. The proportion of imitations was far less in Eric's and Gia's speech, and Allison did not imitate at all. It was also the case that the use of successive single-word utterances was most prevalent in Allison's speech, even though the length of time sampled was considerably smaller. There is, then, some evidence, based on a small sample of only four children, to suggest an inverse relationship between the use of successive single-word utterances and the tendency to imitate.

meat" in (5). There is no way to tell if the subsequent utterances —
after an intervening comment or question — would have occurred
otherwise. But, the fact that certain of the words in succession
occurred in a primitive discourse relation would appear to be
evidence against the naming hypothesis. The second observation
also had to do with discourse relationship. In situations in which a
single utterance was successive to and related to an utterance from
another person, rather than in succession with an utterance of the
child, it appeared that the child's utterance originated with the
other's utterances, rather than as a 'name' for an object, for example,
at 19,2[8]:

II: 60 (19,2)
(A holding the bag of cookies)
   Shall we have a snack?
   Let's sit down and have a snack.
(A going toward the big chair)   chair/

Rather than simply naming objects, it appeared that the children
were talking about the relations in experience among persons,
objects, and events, as in "chair", "pot/ meat", "Mommy/ slipper",
and "car/ see" in the above examples. Their utterances were successive and related to one another by virtue of context and behavior
— they referred to intersecting states of affairs. The lack of sentence prosody and the general unpredictability of the order in which
successive single-word utterances were emitted corresponded with
the observation that the semantic interpretation of such sequences
was totally dependent on context. It was apparent that the children
were aware of and could talk about things that go together, although they were apparently unable to code or specify the relations
among them linguistically.

   Initially, from examples recorded in the diary notes, it appeared

---

[8] In the examples in the text, the Roman numerals refer to the video sessions
I through IV. The numbers after the colon are the numbers of the speech events
in the transcriptions in the Appendix from which the examples were taken. The
numbers in parentheses refer to Allison's age in months and weeks.

that the first word that occurred in a sequence of words referred to the topic or focus of the speech event, and what followed appeared to function as a comment relative to the topic or focus. In the sequence "juice/ more", Allison was talking about the juice, but commenting on or requesting its recurrence; in the sequences "door/ open" and "door/ Mommy", she was talking about the door and commenting on its being opened, or on Mommy opening it. This is essentially the account that had been offered to explain the occurrence of such utterances in the early speech of Gia and Eric[9]. However, such utterances as "more/ juice" and "Mommy/ juice" also occurred, and there were many such sequences recorded in the diary notes in which the distinction between topic and comment was not as readily apparent — for example, "cook/ baby/ pot/ meat" above, and in the following:

(7) (Allison examining a band-aid on
    Daddy's finger)   cut/ Daddy/

Once it was possible to capture the occurrence of successive single-word utterances on video tape and to watch and listen, over and over again, to the speech events in which they occurred, it became apparent that the Topic-Comment account of the structure of successive single-word utterances (coding the relation between 'given' and 'new' aspects of an event), was inadequate as either a description or an explanation of their occurrence. First, in the examples recorded on video tape, it appeared that it was NOT always the topic or 'given' element in a situation that was stated first. In many instances, the first utterance referred to the aspect of the situation that was 'new'. In the following example:

II: 63 (19,2)
(A offering cookie to M)   Mommy/
    Oh, thank you.
(M taking cookie)   cookie/

---

[9] In Lois Bloom, *Language development*, 1970.

Allison commented on the 'new' or 'relational' aspect of the cookie first and then named the topic utterance. See, also, examples in the events II: 38 (in contrast with 47), 63, 64, 77, 88 in the second sample at 19,2; and the events III: 3, 11, 15, 16, 24, 29, 31, 36, 42, 52, 53, 55, 63, 65, 88 in the third sample at 20,3. It appeared, then, that the order of mention of 'given' and 'new' components was essentially variable for the events recorded on video tape.

A careful examination of the sequence of Allison's movements, in relation to what she said, in each of the speech events with successive single-word utterances, revealed two possible event structures with occurrence of such utterances. There appeared to be (1) events with CHAINED successive utterances, which occurred with successive movements; and (2) events with HOLISTIC successive utterances, in which the entire situation appeared to be defined to begin with, and utterances were not tied to particular movements or shifts in context. Although both kinds of 'structures' existed in each video sample, there appeared to be a developmental progression from predominantly chained successive single-word utterances to holistic successive single-word utterances in the period from 16 to 21 months.

In the first sample, as mentioned earlier, many of the speech events included only a single utterance that was repeated several times, for example:

I: 48 (16,3)
(A drops book; trying to get on chair)   up/ up/ up/

However, there were also instances in which different utterances occurred and appeared to be related by virtue of shared topic, as in the following two examples:

I: 68 (16,3)
(A reaching under chair; picking up cow)   cow/ cow/ cow/
(A trying to put cow on chair on hind legs)   chair/ chair/
  What's that?
(A giving cow to M to help)   Mama/
  What, darling?

I: 31 (16,3)
(A had put doll in truck)
(A walking to M; giving M doll)   ma ma ma/ Mama wídə/
    What, darling?

                                                   Mama wídə/ baby/
    Oh, what should I do?

                                                   baby/ baby/ ə wídə/
    Oh, poor baby.
(A going over to truck; looking at M and
doll; patting truck)   ə wídə/ ə wídə/ baby/
                                                   ə wídə/

These last two events provided examples of what appeared to be the two different 'structures' underlying the occurrence of successive and related single-word utterances. In the first example (I: 68), Allison picked up the cow, saying "cow", tried to put it on the chair, saying "chair", and then turned to me for help, saying "Mama". Each of the utterances accompanied a particular movement relative to the total event. Single-word utterances in situations like this one appeared to accompany Allison's successive movements and (or) utterances or movements by someone else. Essentially, such successive single-word utterance events presented a 'chaining' of utterances, each of which was somehow occasioned by a shift in context, where topic was held constant, as Allison noticed, remembered, or did something 'new'. Such utterances were temporally chained and were related to one another only to the extent that they were accompaniments of movements that were temporally and schematically related to one another.

    The underlying 'structure' of utterances in the second example (I: 31) appeared to be different. From Allison's behavior, the context, and her utterances with "Mama" and "baby", it was clear that Allison wanted me to put the doll into the truck. In effect, all of these utterances 'referred' to MAMA putting the DOLL in the truck, although interpretation of Allison's intention was maximally dependent on the context (and, at the time, what she wanted was not clear to me until she went over to the truck and 'gestured' the rest of the situation). In events such as this, Allison seemed to have an entire event in mind at the outset. Her successive utterances were related to one another by virtue of their relation to the total event to which they referred. Moreover, the event was not in the immediate context as such. The successive utterances were related to one another in that they referred to the mental representation of a set of intersecting relations in an immediately anticipated event, in I: 31, in which Mama would act on an object in a particular way.

Both chained and holistic structures were present in the second and third samples. Following are two examples of CHAINED structures from the second sample at 19,2:

II: 51 (19,2)
(A pushes truck past M, off rug; stands up)

                              uh!/
(A pulling truck back on to rug)   back/
  Back.
(A struggling to pull truck onto rug)   up/
  Off?
(A getting truck onto rug)   there/ up/
  On?
(A pulling truck closer)   on/
(A standing up)   there!/

II: 88 (19,2)
(A bounces doll up and down as M had done; stops; holding doll out, looking into empty cup)   bath/
  Bath.
(A bouncing doll in cup again)   bath/
(A picking up imaginary soap from floor) scrub/
(A 'scrubbing' doll's head)   scrub/
  Scrub, scrub.

                              baby/

Baby. Scrub, scrub.

Each of these utterances is chained inasmuch as each accompanied a particular movement by Allison with the truck or doll. Although she no doubt had a goal in mind at the beginning, there appeared to be a shifting of goals within the event. Allison's utterances accompanied her acting out a schema, as "an integral part of it", as has been described by Piaget[10]. In contrast, in the following two examples of the holistic structure of successive single-word utterances, Allison appears to have the whole goal in mind from the outset, and appears to be talking about the complete schema:

II: 80 (19,2)

(A picking up blanket;	blanket/
handing blanket to M)	cover/
Blanket? Cover?	
(A touches doll's head)	
	head/
(A touching doll's head, lifting doll to her	
own head)	head/
(A touching doll's head in front of her)	head/ head/
Head?	
	cover/

II: 27 (19,2)

(A putting horse on chair)	there/
(A having trouble getting horse on chair;	
M reaching out to help)	Mommy/
I'll help. Okay, Mommy'll help you.	
(A trying to put horse on chair)	help/
(no room for horse, A giving it to M)	horse/ help/
Help?	
(A pointing to space on chair)	over there/

Although there were examples of both kinds of event structures in the second and third samples, the holistic successive single-word utterance events came to predominate in the sample at 19,2 and even more so at 20,3, as in the following:

---

[10] Jean Piaget, *Play, dreams and imitation in childhood*, 1951, 223.

III: 90 (20,3)
(A had been wiping her own bottom with
a napkin; A goes to doll on M's lap; wip-
ing doll with napkin)   Mommy baby/
(A giving doll to M)   Mommy/ wiping/
                                               Mommy/ wiping/
(M taking doll)   wiping/
    Wiping what?
(A reaching for doll's bottom)   here/
    Here?
(A wipes doll's bottom)

III: 3 (20,3)
(M had suggested taking off A's coat)
(A pointing to her neck)   up/ up/
    What?

                                               neck/ up/
    Neck? What do you want? What?

                                               neck/
    What's on your neck?
(A pointing to zipper and lifting up her
chin)   zip/ zip/ up/

From her speech and behavior, and the context, it was clear that
Allison wanted me to wipe the doll's bottom, and, in the second
example, zip up her coat, and she appeared to have the whole picture in mind from the outset. In such events there was a distinct
beginning and an end. One has the impression, particularly when
watching a replay of the event, that the entire sequence of utterances
was, essentially, predetermined by Allison's mental representation
of the situation from the beginning.

   CHAINED successive single-word utterances appeared to accompany performance of schemas, as Allison commented on alternative or successive steps towards a goal which could shift, depending on the outcome of her movements. The chaining of utterances
in such events coincides with Piaget's description of the child's

ability, in the first half of the second year, to begin to use alternative means (successive and coordinated schemas) for "giving a meaning to fortuitous events". Such utterances that occurred were related (and successive) by virtue of the fact that they accompanied or commented on Allison's successive, alternative, and coordinated movements. The HOLISTIC successive single-word utterances appeared to occur with a mental representation of the complete schema from the outset, and movements and utterances were directed towards the anticipated schema. Development towards this holistic structure coincided with the development of what Piaget has called the interiorization of actions as the child becomes capable of a mental representation of actions prior to (or instead of) their performance in this same period of time.[11]

The ability to mentally represent a complete action, object, or goal would be a necessary condition for the eventual ability to psychologically coordinate several aspects of an event for formulating the underlying semantic basis of a sentence. As pointed out by Roger Brown:

... there is a fundamental difference of intellectual level between the sensori-motor schema and the semantic intention, or proposition, that gives rise to a sentence. ... It seems likely to me that there is hidden progress in the latter part of the sensori-motor period from the schema that is performed to the schema that is represented mentally to the proposition that is thought and eventually expressed. It may be that multi-word utterances wait upon the accomplishment of this progress.[12]

Allison's single-word utterances were apparently mapped onto successive movements first, and then, subsequently, successive single-word utterances were mapped onto the mental representation of a whole event (object or relation) in experience. She was saying only one word at a time throughout this period from 16 to 21 months, because she had not learned to coordinate and hold in mind at once the several notions underlying her separate UTTERANCES. But, further, she needed to learn the code for mapping her

[11]   Jean Piaget, *Psychology of intelligence*, 1960, 104-105.
[12]   Roger Brown, "*A first language*", in prep.

mental representations of the intersecting relations among objects and people onto the semantic-syntactic relations among words.

Looking back, with the benefit of hindsight, it is probable that the diary examples of successive single-word utterances from Allison (not recorded on tape), as well as the examples recorded on audio tape from Eric, Gia, and Jane, differed among one another in the same respects. Unfortunately, the features of movement and behavior which revealed the proposed distinction between CHAINED and HOLISTIC successive single-word utterance events could not be recorded in audio sessions,. much less hand-recorded in the situations in which they occurred.

There is still no immediate explanation of what determined the order of mention in these events. Factors of focus, salience, or relative importance were no doubt involved, but these aspects of events could not be readily defined in the data. Several things were clear, however. Successive single-word utterances presented evidence of awareness of the intersection of different aspects of a situation. The relations among the separate utterances were a function of the relations among the different aspects of behavior and context in perceived or mentally represented events. There was no evidence for postulating a matching between the successive utterances and an underlying linguistic (sentence) representation.

The use of successive single-word utterances did not characterize the speech of Gia, Eric, Jane, and Allison to the same extent. However, there is considerable support for the phenomenon of successive single-word utterances in the literature — particularly in the diary studies where individual children were observed continuously. Leopold observed "two (related) one-word utterances ... said in succession" just before the emergence of two-word combinations in his daughter's speech[13]. Guillaume gave perhaps the clearest account of the same behavior. He described "des formations personnelles consistant en plusieurs mot-phrases juxtaposés dont l'ensemble n'offre aucune unité grammaticale. ... les mots sont separés par des silences, chacun porte son accent propre."[14] He

[13] Werner Leopold, *Speech development of a bilingual child*, Vol. 3, 1949, 20.
[14] "personal [that is, spontaneous, non-imitated] formations composed of

interpreted such successive single-words as separate holophrases, a series of word-sentences, each of which could stand as a sentence — rather than as an element of a single statement. Whether each word in such a series is interpretable by an adult as a sentence or as an element of a sentence is unimportant. What is important is the impressive evidence of the child's awareness of relationships among aspects of the situation and his obvious inability to code those relationships linguistically.[15]

The use of successive single-word utterances appeared to indicate that the children recognized more than one aspect of a referent, or recognized the relationship between aspects of a referent, before they could use a linguistic code for expressing such cooccurrence or relationship. Once the children named both aspects of a relationship — such as both "door" and "Mommy" when Mommy opened the door, and both "slipper" and "Mommy" when the child saw Mommy's slipper — the evidence for concluding that the words reflected an underlying conceptual relation was stronger than in the same situation with only one utterance. However, it is difficult to specify, first, just what the nature of those conceptual relations is, and, also, what kind of further evidence could be obtained for identifying underlying conceptions in order to distinguish them from linguistic representations.

However, what is obvious is that the words that occurred in such successive single-word utterances were just the kinds of words — indeed, they were very often the SAME words — that are subsequently used in coding the conceptual relations that have been identified in early sentences. Words signalling the notions of existence, nonexistence, disappearance, and recurrence ("there", "no", "away", "gone", and "more") occurred and object names occurred. Both

---

several juxtaposed word-sentences which — taken together — have no grammatical unity ... the words are separated by pauses and each one has its own stress." Paul Guillaume, "Les débuts de la phrase chez l'enfant", *Journal de Psychologie*, 1927.

[15] See also, Oscar Bloch, "La phrase dans le langage de l'enfant", *Journal de Psychologie*, 1924; Joshua Smith, "The development and structure of holophrases", 1970.

action words and person names occurred successively with object names in situations where objects were acted upon and people did things or were otherwise associated with objects. In short, the children presented evidence of a realization of certain conceptual relations among objects and events in experience, and it was obvious that they had yet to discover the way in which the language they had been exposed to coded such basic notions in terms of semantic-syntactic relationship among words.

One thing was abundantly clear, however. An hypothesis of insufficient vocabulary could not account for the nonoccurrence of sentences. The children certainly used enough words for sentences; in fact, they used precisely the words in succession which they could be expected to combine in two-word utterances eventually. Thus, they knew enough words to talk about more than one aspect of an event or relation, but they did not use syntax. If, indeed, the children's single-word utterances were 'sentences' or 'holophrases', why did sentences not occur — given that the children could actually say two word forms together (as with Allison's "wídə"), they knew enough different words, and they differentiated aspects of an event? The reason why sentences did not occur — and the reason why their single-word utterances cannot accurately be characterized as 'sentences' — is that the children did not as yet know the LINGUISTIC CODE for mapping conceptual notions onto semantic-syntactic relations in sentences.

3.3. COMPREHENSION AND SYNTAX

Children learn that objects are acted upon, that people or movable objects do things, that objects and events exist, cease to exist, and recur. This is the basis of perceptual-cognitive experience in the early years, and so it should not be surprising that these are the kinds of things that children talk about in early speech. But whereas children need to learn a linguistic code for talking about such phenomena as relations among objects and events in the world, knowledge of the code is not necessary for their understanding

such relations. Such phenomenological relations simply exist —
without a dependence on linguistic form — in the context and
behavior of events and states in early experience. The child's
developing perception and cognitive awareness somehow organize
his experience so that categories of events and states of affairs come
to be discriminated and conceptually represented.

A principal source of evidence used to substantiate the counter-
claim — that children use their knowledge of linguistic form to
organize experience and then talk about it — is the assumption that
children understand structural relations in sentences after 12
months and certainly well before two years of age. However, several
observations of children can be cited to argue that this is probably
not the case.

Children between one and two years of age do appear to understand a great deal that is said to them — often responding appropriately to complex statements. But the directions and statements
they respond to so readily refer to their immediately perceptible
experience more often than not. It has often been pointed out that
children's early utterances are very much tied to the context and
behavior in the speech events in which they occur. There is an
overwhelming redundancy in children's early speech in relation to
context and behavior — children talk about what they see and do.
It should not be surprising that children are dependent on the
support of the situation for comprehension in much the same way.
Utterances in the speech of mothers addressed to children are
frequently redundant in relation to context and behavior, and
language learning no doubt depends on the relation between the
speech the child hears and what he sees and does.

It remains to be tested whether children using single-word utterances understand sentences in non-redundant contexts as well as
they understand what is said to them about what they can see or
hear, or what they do, aside from often repeated and familiar
phrases. If they do not understand sentences that refer to relations
among objects and events that are not immediately available, then
the extent to which they analyze syntactic structure in their understanding is certainly questionable. Such skepticism about early

comprehension has been voiced often[16]. Leopold concluded that comprehension at this age depends primarily on the child's recognizing the highly stressed, salient words of an utterance. Adults speaking to children repeat and vary the form of their messages by exaggerating prosody to emphasize key words to help the child to understand. Guillaume vividly described the elaborations through gesture, emphasis, and repetition that are necessary to help very young children understand what is said to them[17]. Probably such cues come to be automatic for the adult, and children no doubt come to look for such cues, and to use them efficiently in getting meaning from the stream of speech that they hear.

The principal empirical evidence that exists in support of the claim of prior comprehension before production of certain syntactic structures has to do exclusively with children older than the children discussed here. The studies of Fraser, Bellugi, and Brown with three-year-olds and Lovell and Dixon with two-year-olds produced similar results and appeared to demonstrate that children understand certain linguistic structures before they use them[18]. More recently, however, Fernald[19] has cast doubt on this claim. He equated the response possibilities for both comprehension and production in the Fraser, Bellugi, and Brown experimental tasks, by not considering trials that produced irrelevant responses in production. Irrelevancies had been scored as errors by Fraser, Bellugi, and Brown. That is, when looking only at correct or incorrect responses

[16]   See, for example, Renira Huxley, "Discussion", in John Lyons and Roger Wales (eds.), *Psycholinguistics papers*, 1966, 210-211; Carlota Smith, "An experimental approach to children's linguistic competence", in John Hayes (ed.), *Cognition and the development of language*, 1970, 118; and Martin D. S. Braine, "On two types of models of the internalization of grammars", in Dan I. Slobin (ed.), *The ontogenesis of grammar*, 1971.

[17]   Paul Guillaume, "Les debuts de la phrase dans le langage de l'enfant", 1927.

[18]   Colin Fraser, Ursula Bellugi, and Roger Brown, "Control of grammar in imitation, comprehension and production", 1963; K. Lovell and E. M. Dixon, "The growth of the control of grammar in imitation, comprehension and production", *Journal of Child Psychology and Psychiatry*, 1967.

[19]   Charles Fernald, "Children's active and passive knowledge of syntax", 1970.

in both kinds of tasks, comprehension and production were essentially the same.

In a series of experiments with older children and adults, Huttenlocher has consistently demonstrated that comprehension of a statement — as measured by the ability to create a corresponding arrangement of objects — is influenced by variations in the nonlinguistic state of affairs presented along with the statement. For example, there are important differences in response to the statement "the red truck is pushing the green truck", depending on whether one or the other or neither of the trucks is already placed on a three space track[20]. If adults and older children are so influenced by differences in nonlinguistic context in their responses to the same utterance, then it is not difficult to assume that very young children are as dependent for comprehension, if not more so, on cues in the nonlinguistic contexts in which utterances occur naturally.

Finally, there is the study by Shipley, Smith, and Gleitman, that reported comprehension data for children using single-word utterances. When presented with commands that were alternatively single words, 'telegraphic', or well-formed, children who use only single words responded most often to single word commands.[21]

The crucial difference then between comprehension and expression is not that the one precedes the other — that children somehow learn to decode linguistic structure before they are able to use linguistic structure in talking. Rather, they do not need to know

[20]   Janellen Huttenlocher and Susan Weiner, "Comprehension of instructions in varying contexts", *Cognitive Psychology*, 1971. See, also, Janellen Huttenlocher and Susan Strauss, "Comprehension and a statement's relation to the situation it describes", *Journal of Verbal Learning and Verbal Behavior*, 1968.
[21]   Elizabeth Shipley, Carlota Smith, and Lila Gleitman, "A study in the acquisition of language", 1969. This result was in apparent contrast to a second group of children who used 'telegraphic' speech. The older children who were using two and three-word utterances responded better to well-formed commands than to 'telegraphic' or single-word commands. However, this second result cannot be taken as evidence that comprehension exceeds production — if the well-formed commands were essentially the same syntactic structure represented in the children's 'telegraphic', that is, reduced, utterances. It was pointed out in Lois Bloom, *Language development*, 1970, that early two-word utterances were often reductions of more complete or complex underlying structure.

syntax in order to understand when someone talks about the contextual relations between Mommy and Baby and eating and getting and ball and carrots and pudding, when such objects and events occur along with utterances. There are certain adult semantic constraints on such words as "Mommy", "eat", "get", "carrots", and "ball" which characterize restrictions on the occurrence of words relative to one another in adult sentences. Knowledge of such semantic constraints and knowledge of syntax are necessary for understanding linguistic messages that do not refer to the contexts in which they occur. In such utterances, the 'meaning' is in the linguistic message alone. But when a sentence is redundant with respect to the context in which it occurs, then the amount of information which the child needs to get from the linguistic message is probably minimal.

Children do need to learn something about the syntax of the language and semantic constraints in order to talk about such conceptual relations in any coherent way. And they need to analyze the speech they hear in relation to what they see and do in order to learn its structure. This perceptual-cognitive analysis of linguistic and nonlinguistic experience results in the child's learning the structure of language — but the extent to which he has done this before he uses syntax in his speech is open to serious question. If, indeed, children's early understanding of speech can be shown to be maximally dependent on context and other extra-linguistic cues (such as repetition, exaggeration, gesture, etc.), then the argument — that children (1) give evidence of understanding 'sentences' and so (2) know something about sentence structure before they say sentences, and therefore (3) single-word utterances are sentences — becomes far less convincing. If children do not use linguistic structure to process the sentences that they hear, then their 'understanding' of messages cannot be taken as evidence that single-word utterances are holophrastic.

3.4. EARLY PROSODY AND SYNTAX

Both rising and falling intonations have been observed in children's earliest vocalizations even before words are identified in the second half of the first year. Such intonation contours have often been compared with the question and statement prosody contours of adult sentences. The occurrence of such different intonation contours in early non-speech vocalization and single-word utterances is often taken as evidence of certain prior knowledge of aspects of linguistic structure.[22] However, Weir[23] reported that she was unable to find any systematic differences in the use of different prosody patterns in the syntactic speech of her two-year-old son. Miller and Ervin[24] reported that they were unable to find prosody patterns used contrastively until the development of the grammatical system was well under way after two years of age. There is some question, then, whether the rising and falling intonation patterns in single-word utterances are distinctive in the same way as in the adult model. There is no behavioral evidence reported to indicate that children intend a question or a statement — both prosodic patterns apparently occur in the same situations and contexts.

In an analysis of the sequence of Allison video tapes from 16,3 to 28 months, Lahey observed a marked difference in the occurrence of sentence prosody contours.[25] In the first tape, at 16,3, utterances with "wíd∂" and the few other utterances with words in juxtaposition (for example, with "more" and "away") occurred with unequal stress and without intervening pause between the words or terminal falling contour after the first word. That is, such juxtaposed words af 16,3 occurred with apparent sentence prosody. In the second and third video samples at 19,2 and 20,3, successive single words occurred, separated by pauses, each with terminal falling contours.

---

[22]   Most recently, for example, by Paula Menyuk, *Sentences children use*, 1969; Thomas G. Bever, Jerry A. Fodor, and William Weksel, "On the acquisition of syntax: A critique of 'Contextual generalization'", *Psychological Review*, 1965.
[23]   Ruth Weir, "Some questions on the child's learning of phonology", in Frank Smith and George Miller (eds.), *The genesis of language*, 1966.
[24]   Wick Miller and Susan Ervin, "The development of grammar in child language", in Ursula Bellugi and Roger Brown (eds.), *The acquisition of language*, 1964.
[25]   Margaret Lahey, "The role of prosody and syntactic markers in children's comprehension of spoken sentences", 1972.

However, the few instances of words in juxtaposition (which were fewer at 19,2 than at 16,3) were not produced with the same sentence prosody as had been heard at 16,3. In the fourth sample, at 22 months, the use of syntax was unmistakable, and such utterances occurred as "wiping Baby chin" (as Allison wiped her chin) and "Baby Allison comb hair" (as Allison put her hand to her hair). All of the combinations at 19,2; 20,3; and 22 months were produced slowly and with more equal stress on each word. They were distinguished as sentences from the successive single-word utterances described earlier by falling intonation indicating terminal contour after the last word only (and not each of the words) and shorter (but somewhat variable) pause time between the words.

Lahey concluded that such early sentences at 20,3 and 22 months did not occur with sentence prosody — in contrast with utterances with "wídə" at 16,3 and later sentences at 28 months. She has suggested that children may mimic adult prosody patterns (apparently well before their first birthday) and use variable prosody patterns with single-word utterances in much the same way as they babble different sound patterns before learning the phonological contrasts for word distinction. The lack of sentence prosody at 20,3 and 22 months — when Allison was learning to use syntax — and the subsequent appearance of sentence prosody in her speech by 28 months would indicate that children learn to use prosody patterns in their speech after they learn that basic grammatical distinctions are signaled by word order in English, that is, after they learn to use syntax. It would appear then that the occurrence of question, statement, and exclamation contours in the use of single-word utterances cannot be taken as unequivocal evidence of an inherent notion of 'sentence' as has sometimes been suggested.

In summary, single-word utterances are not sentences. Children in the first half of the second year do not use phrases and sentences — they say only one word at a time. When single-word utterances are successive, within the bounds of a single speech event, there is some evidence to indicate that the child is aware of relational aspects of experience. But children do not use syntax — utterances are largely unpredictable relative to one another — and there is no evidence from their linguistic performance that children 'know' the semantic-syntactic structure of the language that they hear.

It is apparent that children cannot productively use two words together within the bounds of a single utterance. The evidence from Allison indicated that this constraint was not a factor of motor immaturity — utterances with the mysterious "wídə" at 16 months were two 'words' long. There are no data on memory capacity at this age, but there is some doubt that the limit to one word at a time is a limitation on processes of recall. For one thing, the children gave no indication that they had 'forgotten' parts of an otherwise longer utterance when they said only one word, such as "Mommy" or "more". Moreover, utterances with "wídə" and the utterances with two words in juxtaposition at 16,3 (Table 3, p. 44) presented evidence of memory for certain primitive order relations between words. Further, with respect to presumed 'comprehension', children's response to statements and directions at this age may well be a function of the redundancy of linguistic messages relevant to the corresponding states of affairs in immediate contexts. Children do not need to analyze the structure of such utterances in order to respond or 'understand' what is expected of them. Finally, differences in the prosody of single words may somehow function differently in the child's speech than in the adult model, and may be a manifestation of the ability to mimic superficial aspects of adult speech.

With regard to this last point, there appear to be several superficial features of speech which children show evidence of discriminating and 'using' without obvious intention or motivation. The period of babbling in infancy is usually described as one in which the child discriminates and produces different sounds that approximate speech sounds, but babbling is generally conceded to be pre-linguistic behavior. Such sounds that the child produces are not tied to any aspect of meaning; they are non-contrastive; they are not phonemic. The use of prosodic features of intonation and stress in extended, unintelligible vocalization and with single words appears to be another instance of the use of an aspect of speech behavior without linguistic motivation or contrast. That is, different prosody contours in this period of time may not distinguish the meanings or functions of utterances from one another. Finally, Allison's use of "wídə" was taken as evidence of a similar use of a superficial feature of speech, in this case, word order.

There is some evidence then that features of prosody and features of syntax can be reproduced and 'practiced' by the child in much the same way as he babbles sounds before he learns phonemic contrasts in words. But just as the child needs to learn many of the sounds he had babbled when he learns to say words[26], he also needs to learn prosody distinctions as supra-segmental features of syntax — after he learns something about syntax; and he also needs to learn syntactic word order after he learns something about the meaning relations among words. Thus, the same or similar pre-linguistic behaviors — with phonology, prosody, and syntax — need to be 'relearned' by the child at some later time as linguistic mechanisms, that is, as language behavior for coding meaning.

In addition to the constraint of not knowing the form of language or the code, there is also the possibility of a psychological limitation on the ability to coordinate two or more aspects of an event to formulate a proposition for the semantic basis of a sentence. It may be for just this reason that children do not simply string together their single words within a single utterance before they learn syntax. Alternatively, it is conceivable that a child might coordinate two or more concepts in a proposition of a sentence and still not map such coordinate concepts onto structured sentences. This might account for those instances where order in early English sentences was apparently free and not predictable, as has been reported, for example, by Braine[27].

It appears then that children say only one word at a time primarily because they do not yet know the linguistic code. Although no doubt cognizant of certain relations in experience, they are unable to code such experience linguistically. But, although children

---

[26]   As described by Roman Jakobson, *Child language, aphasia and phonological universals*, 1968.

[27]   Martin D. S. Braine, "The acquisition of language in infant and child", in Carroll Reed (ed.), *The learning of language*, 1970.

are evidently aware of intersecting aspects of situations and states of affairs, it is not at all clear what the nature of their conceptual representations of such relationships might be. Mental structures, concepts, or schemas evolve slowly out of the child's many interactions with objects and events; they are never static, but necessarily change as the child matures and his interactions with his environment extend to new and different objects and events. There were situations in all four of the video sessions in which Allison made reference to what appeared to be the same or similar relation. For example, in I (28), Allison reached for Mama's juice and said "Mama"; in II (66), Allison pointed to Mommy's cup and said "juice/Mommy"; in III (45), Allison gave a cup to Mommy saying "Mommy juice"; and in IV (15) Allison was eating Mommy's cookie and said "eat Mommy cookie". In each of these events Allison was talking about an object in what might be called the 'possessive' relation to Mommy. But, it was most probably not the case that the underlying concept or schema of Mommy in relation to certain objects was the same in all four events, much less that the words she used had the same 'semantic structure'.

The evidence presented thus far appears to indicate that the child's conceptual representation of events does not depend on or derive from a linguistic basis — that is, such conceptual representation does not take the form of such 'constructs' as basic grammatical relations or semantic structures, if both GRAMMATICAL and SEMANTIC refer to the representation of linguistic categories and their interrelations.

4

DEVELOPMENTAL CHANGE IN THE USE OF SINGLE-WORD UTTERANCES

The use of single-word utterances is usually described as the first of the 'developmental milestones' in language acquisition. But the essence of development is CHANGE and there has been an unfortunate tendency to overlook inherent variation in this period which might provide evidence of what children are learning in the course of this stage of development. It has generally been assumed in the literature that children simply accumulate a number of different words (that are most often noun forms in the adult model) until they begin to combine them into phrases. But what of the kinds of words that are used and the ways in which they are used in this period of time? It would be surprising if the only difference between the child of 12-13 months, the child of 15-16 months, and the child of 18-19 months was in the numbers of different words understood or used. Specifically, to look for the origins of grammar, one would like to be able to explain how the use of single words at one point in time is immediately antecedent to the use of syntax, whereas the use of single words at an earlier time is evidently not. The child of 13-14 months is usually not about to use syntax, whereas the child of 19-20 months frequently is.

4.1. THE DISTINCTION BETWEEN CLASSES OF SINGLE WORDS

The kinds of words that Allison used before she used syntax could be differentiated in at least two ways. To begin with, it was possible to study the distribution of different words in terms of relative frequency of occurrence and persistence of use. One could also describe the words in terms of their referential function — that is, their use in situations that had or did not have certain features in common.

4.1.1. The Frequency and Relative Persistence of Different Words

Allison's increasing use of new words in the period from 9 to 18 months did not result in a cumulative vocabulary or lexicon. That is, certain words were used for a time and then no longer used. One might expect that once a word is used by a child with some regularity in appropriate situations, then the word would continue to be used as similar situations recurred. This was not the case in the course of Allison's development[1]. By the age of 14 months, over 25 different words had been heard in Allison's speech; however, within a one-week period there were never more than 10 to 12 different words occurring with regularity. The 25 different words she used from 9 to 14 months each occurred more than once, with consistent and recognizable form, over a period of at least several days. However, many words dropped from use and did not reappear until several or many months later. In some instances, the word reappeared with different phonetic or lexical form. For example, the word for *flower* at 14 months was [gə́jə̀]; at 18 months the word for *flower* reappeared as [fáwə̀]. The word "dog" occurred from 12 to 13 months, and reappeared as "bowwow" at 19 months[2]. It was not

---

[1] Leopold reported a "mortality" for words in this same period of time in his daughter's speech (Vol. 1, 159-160); Oscar Bloch also reported that words dropped out of use and reappeared at a later time in the development of his three children ("Premiers stades du langage de l'enfant", *Journal de Psychologie*, 1921); and Dorothea McCarthy referred to reports of both cumulative and non-cumulative vocabularies in early development ("Language development in children", 1954, 526). The disuse of words after their initial appearance may explain why growth of vocabulary before the last half of the second year is often described as slow. See, for example, John Carroll. *Language and thought*, 1964, 32; Eric Lenneberg, *Biological foundations of language*, 1967, 131; and Dorothea McCarthy, "Language development in children", 1954, 527.

[2] Bloch reported that such words that dropped out were different in form when they reappeared, reflecting the children's more recent phonological development ("Premiers stades du langage de l'enfant", 1921).

possible, at the time, to discern any reason why such words ceased to be used. For example, "dog" occurred originally when Allison (1) saw a dog or different dogs, or (2) heard a dog bark, or (3) heard the clinking of a dog's identification tags. All of these experiences continued to occur. Allison both saw and heard dogs; she simply did not say the word in the same situations[3].

However, there was a small group of words that Allison continued to use persistently and far more frequently than any other words in this same period of time from 9 to 17 or 18 months. This group of words included names of people — "Mama", "Dada", "Mimi" (her baby sitter) and "Baby" (both in reference to herself and to other babies and to her dolls). All of these names of people had first occurred before 12 months. The remaining words that were used frequently and that persisted were "there", "up", "uh oh", "no", "away", "gone", "stop", and "more". Table 4 presents all of the words that occurred in the video tape sample of Allison's speech at age 16, 3 with the frequency of occurrence for each. The seven most frequent words (occurring at least 19 times) accounted for 65% of all single word utterances in the 40-minute sample.

Clearly, there was a small group of words that Allison used more frequently than other words. These words also tended to be used continually after their initial appearance. At the same time, there was a large number of different words that occurred relatively less frequently, with a tendency for some words to drop from use as

---

[3] Allison did not spontaneously repeat the speech of others, that is, she did not imitate. She did not attempt to imitate when asked to and she was not pressed to do so. It is worth considering the possibility that children who do not appear to stop saying words after their initial use — that is, children whose lexical acquisition is apparently 'cumulative' in the first half of the single-word utterance period — are also children who spontaneously imitate or repeat utterances that they hear. Their using a word with apparent persistence may simply reflect this propensity to repeat a word heard in a previous utterance — with or without some intervening delay. That is, they use the word because they have just heard it used in a particular context. Both Allison and Hildegard Leopold did not spontaneously imitate, and both used words that did not persist in active use. This connection between the tendency to imitate and the relative persistence of different words is necessarily speculative but it is not unreasonable.

TABLE 4

Single-Word Utterances and their Frequency of Occurrence
Allison at 16 months, 3 weeks

all gone, 1	there, 30
away, 9	turn, 1
baby, 19	uh, 2
car, 2	uh oh, 7
chair, 14	up, 27
cookie, 15	wídə, 1
cow, 3	
Dada, 4	
dirty, 2	
down, 22	
girl, 3	
gone, 19	
here, 1	
horse, 1	Most Frequent: there, 30
Mama, 9	up, 27
mess, 2	more, 24
more, 24	down, 22
no, 21	no, 21
oh, 3	gone, 19
pig, 6	baby, 19
sit, 1	
stop, 1	

other words came into use. The relative frequency and endurance
of word-forms was less interesting, however, than how such words
were used — in terms of aspects of the behavior and context in the
speech events in which utterances occurred.

4.1.2. *Referential Function of Single-Word Utterances*

It is commonplace to observe a child use the word "chair" in a
context in which an object for sitting is the focus of the child's
attention, "cookie" in a context in which a specific object for eating
is the focus, and so on. A name of an object, such as "chair", makes
nominal reference to a particular object x, which is a member of a
class of objects X_n that have certain configurational and functional
attributes in common, and which distinguish them from classes of

objects Y_n, Z_n, ... Although the child may use (or recognize) the word-form in reference to only a highly particular instance of the class X_n objects initially, he eventually extends the reference to different objects in different contexts. The basis for this generalization is usually easily recognized — features in common that can be seen, heard, or felt, and the common uses to which the objects can be put (like sitting and eating).

Certain other words in early lexicons do not make reference to classes of objects in the same way. The word "more" was first used by Allison when she was 16 months old and occurred in a situation in which she had frequently heard the word — during a meal, when offered a second portion of food, after she had already eaten a first portion. Two days after she had first used "more" to request the recurrence of food, she used the word to request her baby sitter to tickle her again, after having been tickled just previously. Subsequently, "more" also referred to another instance of an object in the presence of the original object; for example, Allison pointed to one shoe, commented "shoe", and then pointed to the second shoe and commented "more".

What are the features of context and behavior that would lead a child to extend the meaning of a word like "more" to refer to aspects of objects and events (like meat, tickling, and shoes) that, in themselves, differ from one another both perceptually and functionally? It is necessary for the child to perceive that such classes of objects or events as X_n, Y_n, Z_n, ... have certain repeating behaviors in common — for example, they exist, cease to exist, and recur in his experience. The word-form "more" refers not to instances of phenomena a_1, a_2, ... of a class of phenomena A_n. Rather, the instances a_1, a_2, ..., a_n are α instances of x_1, x_2, ..., X_n, Y_n, Z_n, ... objects and events. Thus, "more" is an inherently relational term — its meaning extends to and depends upon, in every instance, an aspect of behavior of some object or event in the environment. But the object or event has a status in the child's experience that is also independent of the 'meaning' of "more".

Thus, the meaning of certain word-forms such as "more", "up", "no", "away" is inherently relational or transitive, which is essentially what Ingram attempted to account for in his description of the alternative uses of "up" by Leopold's daughter, Hildegard[4]. A word like "up" occurs in situations that vary with respect to different people as agents and different things as objects. But the meaning of "up" (or "more") does not depend on the agent-object relationship, as Ingram implied, but only on a specific aspect of their behavioral interaction, namely, the NOTION of 'upness' (or the NOTION of RECURRENCE). Thus, it is also true that "up" refers to static conditions — for example, a book up on the shelf, where the agent does not matter at all. Another instance of a shoe, or "more shoe", does not necessarily involve an agent or anything else other than the prior or simultaneous occurrence of the same object or one very similar to it. The child comes to recognize recurrent phenomena — in certain instances the figurative and functional attributes of phenomena like chairs and shoes, in other instances behavioral or relational phenomena like the notions 'upness', disappearance, or recurrence with respect to objects like chairs and shoes. Both kinds of phenomena come to be represented by the child as conceptual notions that can be conveniently coded by word-forms.

Thus, one way to differentiate among kinds of words in early pre-syntax lexicons has to do with referential function. When one considers the range of phenomena to which a particular utterance by the child refers, it is possible to distinguish two kinds of word-forms: SUBSTANTIVE forms which make reference to classes of objects and events that are discriminated on the basis of their perceptual features or attributes, and FUNCTION or relational forms which make reference across such perceptually distinguished classes of objects and events.

4.2. THE DEVELOPMENT OF SUBSTANTIVE WORDS

SUBSTANTIVE forms make reference to X_n, Y_n, Z_n ... classes of objects, for example, chairs and cookies. Such words as "chair" and

[4]   David Ingram, "Transitivity in child language", 1971.

"cookie" are 'relational' only to the extent that a particular object is a "chair" or a "cookie" by virtue of its phenomenological relationship to other instances of similar objects (positive relation) or dissimilar objects (negative relation). However, before the child can learn such relations among different objects, he has had to notice that there are properties of his environment which simply exist — which are there and which share certain features of having shape, location in space, and movement. There are, then, objects in general which have configuration and relative proximity, and which can move or be moved.

Children often present evidence in their earliest use of words of this simple awareness of the fact of objects: that whatever they can touch, hold, drop, throw, push, see, and hear exists — is "this" or "thing". Leopold has explicitly described the use of demonstrative forms in Hildegard's speech. A "demonstrative interjection" [ʔət] occurred from age 8 months and was replaced by [dɛ], "*there* ... a pure demonstrative without interrogative intonation*", at 10 months. Both occurred with pointing gestures in a variety of situations. In turn, [dɛ] was replaced, at 12 months, by [da] which was the form that prevailed, with abundant use, until it was replaced by "this" at 18 months. Leopold reported that "demonstratives similar to [da] are frequent in the early speech of children in different countries. *Cf.*, *e.g.* [da], [ta] of a French child [reported by] Grégoire ..."[5]

Allison used a deictic form [ət] from 13 to 14 months. The 'sound' was accompanied by pointing (or, less often, touching) and occurred with great frequency for approximately one month. The form "there" was recorded in Allison's speech at 15 months as an apparent comment on the existence of objects (with and without pointing). It also occurred in a routine, after "Where's _____?" from someone else. I do not have records of an earlier use of demonstrative forms such as those described at length by Leopold. I did not attend closely to the evolution of speech forms from babbling sounds as did Leopold, and it may well be that Allison used a primitive

⁵ Werner Leopold, *Speech development of a bilingual child*, Vol. 1, 1939, 61, 71, 73 and 81.

demonstrative form that was phonetically variable or otherwise not coherent. 'Interjections' have often been reported among children's first words, and such 'words' often appear to accompany notice of an object or event and may have similar deictic or demonstrative function.

Certain things of which the child becomes aware are more like one another than they are like other things: some things move and others do not; some things make noise and others do not; some things are sat upon and others are not. The early and primitive organization of such perceptual and functional features of objects would appear to be a prerequisite for the child to begin to make reference to objects, and eventually to use such words as "cookie" and "chair". Substantive words, then, develop with 'word-image' representations for the child — to the extent that the use of the form depends upon his experience with figurative features which certain kinds of particular OBJECTS in his experience have in common.

The word the child uses clearly does not make reference to precisely the same range of phenomena as in the adult use of the word. There are instances of both UNDER-INCLUSION and OVER-INCLUSION. On the one hand, the child may use a word only in a highly specific instance of occurrence of the referent — as, for example, Allison's early use of "car" at 9 months to refer only to a car moving by on the street below, as she watched from the living room window. At 9 and 10 months she did not say "car" when she was in a car, when she saw a car standing still, or when she saw pictures of cars. Moreover, she did not say "car" again until approximately five months later, at which time it occurred in all of these contexts after its reappearance in her speech.[6]

Instances of OVER-INCLUSION appear to be of two kinds. The first is one in which a number of different phenomena come to be

---

[6] Oscar Bloch reported that the early use of those words that did not persist in his children's speech tended to be over-extended before they dropped out. When they subsequently reappeared in the children's speech they were used in a stricter sense ("Premiers stades du langage de l'enfant", *Journal de Psychologie*, 1921).

associated by the child on the basis of either or both figurative and functional features of the contexts in which they are perceived. For example, Guillaume[7] described the following referents for "nénin" (breast) as used by his young son: to ask for the breast, also a biscuit; in reference to the red button of a piece of clothing; the point of a bare elbow; an eye in a picture; his mother's face in a photograph. Virtually all of the diary studies in the literature report impressively similar kinds of examples, most typically with the early use of "Mama" and "Papa" or words associated with food or feeding.

There are several important aspects of this first kind of over-inclusion, of which "nénin" has been used as an example. First, reports of such over-inclusion based on a heterogeneous but somehow related (for the child) group of features are recorded in the diary studies as occurring EARLY — among the child's first words — with only a few (usually one or two) different words reported for individual children.

More important, however, the features in the range of referents which APPEAR to be seen as common by the child are not ordinarily seen as such by the adult. It is necessary to look for them and to reflect on why the child might use the same word in such different situations. Also, there appear to be a number of different perceptual and functional features (virtually a 'chaining' of features in the sense described by Vygotsky[8]), that the child has discriminated — for example, in the use of "nénin": roundness and pointedness in addition to food, hunger, and his mother. Werner described "this primitive type of classification as based on a togetherness of different things in a realistic situation". He used as examples the use of "qua-qua" to designate both duck and water, and the use of "afta" to designate drinking glass, a pane of glass, window, and also contents of a glass, and concluded, "in such cases the collective meaning

---

[7] Paul Guillaume, "Les débuts de la phrase dans le langage de l'enfant", 1927. Although no age is specifically reported for this use of "nénin", it occurs in the context of the discussion of "les premiers mots" at about 11 to 12 months.
[8] Lev Vygotsky, *Language and thought*, 1962, 64.

is based on the uniform concrete situations in which all these objects belong."[9] He suggested that such objects are grouped together because they are experienced together. By contrast, the use of "nénin" was not confined to objects experienced together, but, rather, based on some perceptual and functional commonality among events. As with "afta" there are similarities from instance to instance, but there is no common feature in all instances of the use of the word. Brown has commented that such "component resemblances as in the referents for such early words are not inclusive concepts and do not seem to be added together. There is rather an unaccountable shifting from one attribute to another, none of the attributes being fully exploited."[10]

Another kind of extension of reference has been described most succinctly by Brown in reporting the development of the meaning of "fa fa" or "flowers", described originally by Lewis:[11]

The child ... at first listens and observes, then points on request [to flowers] and eventually names new instances. The child's experience of referents is ... distributed and discontinuous in time. Somehow the recurrent word, *flowers* ..., serves to attract relevant experiences, to sum them over time into a conception governing the use of the word. ... The second named instance of flowers, at the age of sixteen months and thirteen days, is the same as the first. Both are yellow jonquils growing in a bowl and so recognition requires only that the child have the conception of AN ENDURING OBJECT [emphasis added]. At this point *flowers* is the name of an 'identity category'. With the next instance the referent becomes an equivalence category. The flowers are of a new species and a different color but still in a bowl. At age 17:24 an immense abstraction is called for. The flowers are pictures in a book, lacking odor, texture and tridimensionality. ... At the end of the record [at 22:26] ... he is correctly labeling embroidered flowers and sugar flowers on a biscuit (p. 311).

The child's use of criterial features to distinguish referents for "fa fa", and to thereby extend the meaning of the word to include the same range of phenomena to which the word "flower" might

---

[9] Heinz Werner, *Comparative psychology of mental development*, 1948, 226.
[10] Roger Brown, *Social psychology*, 1965, 327.
[11] In Roger Brown, *Social psychology*, 1965, 311-312; from M. M. Lewis, *How children learn to speak*, 1959.

refer in adult use, appears to be a later development than the kind of over-inclusion described earlier (with the example "nénin" from Guillaume). It appears to begin sometime toward the second half of the second year, and characterizes much of the 'naming' behavior described often as the developmental phenomenon of 'generalizing to new instances'. Brown observed that "Lewis's account of the development of 'fa fa' does not look like the growth of a chain complex"[12]. He goes on to conclude, however, that it was exactly that — but simply not so reported (that is, incompletely reported) in the diary account. I cannot agree. The descriptions of range of reference for early words in the diary data appear to distinguish two distinctly different phenomena. The EARLY over-inclusion of referents in the use of a particular word (for example, "nénin") appears to represent a loose and shifting association of figurative, functional, or affective features of otherwise diverse objects and events. Generalizing to new instances on the basis of clearly discriminable, consistent, and recurrent features of objects apparently occurs LATER (usually midway through the second year) and characterizes most of the child's use of new and different words.

However, there is a third instance of generalizing to new instances which can be characterized as a second and different sort of over-inclusion (that is, different from the associative chaining of different features of referents as in the example "nénin"). Beginning midway into the second year, but usually continuing well into the school years, children make 'errors' of over-inclusion in which criterial features are used to distinguish classes of objects, but the 'name' given to such objects by the child somehow misses the mark. Examples of such over-inclusions that appear often in the literature are the child's use of "dog" to refer to all four-legged animals, or "truck" to refer to all vehicles. In such instances, children have clearly discriminated a particular perceptual criterion for reference to objects. Although they are 'wrong' — that is, horses are not dogs — they are not so far wrong as in the earlier instances of over-inclusion where the criterial feature was neither so easily identified

---

[12]   Roger Brown, *Social psychology*, 1965, 326.

nor so constant — the point of the elbow or the red button was not "nénin". When children call all four-legged animals "dog" or all vehicles "truck" the criterial feature can be readily perceived and it is relatively consistent across referents.

The child's groping for the commonality of features among objects results in several different kinds of behavior which appear to reflect the alternative ways in which children USE words in reference to objects and events. It is being assumed, then, that something about the meaning which any particular word might have for a child can be inferred from his USE of that word in particular contexts. These manifestations of the development of word-reference-meaning appear to be developmentally ordered and can be represented as three phases: (A) "nénin", (B) "fa fa", and (C) "dog"[13].

Phase (A), "nénin", is the early use of a word to refer to a number of different objects and events which are somehow more or less loosely associated by the child. Each use of the word is apparently unrelated to the others and all of the 'referents' for the words appear to converge only insofar as they share perceptual or functional elements which the CHILD has come to associate together. The 'semantic field' is amorphous so far as the adult range of reference for the same form (or similar form in the case of invented forms, which "nénin" appeared to be) is concerned.

Brown has described phenomena such as "nénin" as the child's formation of "large abstract categories" which come about through a primitive abstraction based on a failure on the part of the child to sufficiently differentiate the features of objects and events[14]. To be sure, the child has not differentiated the referents for "nénin"

---

[13] The source of evidence for the following discussion was, in large part, the nineteenth and twentieth century diary data reported in the literature (in particular, in Paul Guillaume, "Les débuts de la phrase dans le langage de l'enfant", 1927; M. M. Lewis, *Infant speech*, 1951; and Leopold) reinterpreted in view of the evidence obtained from Allison's development in the use of single-word utterances. The conclusions that are offered are necessarily tentative, and form hypotheses which remain to be tested with considerably more evidence than is currently available in any of the existing studies.

[14] Roger Brown, "How shall a thing be called?", *Psychological Review*, 1958.

insofar as his USE of the word is concerned. But it is not clear that he does not perceptually discriminate among the objects to which he refers — regardless of what he calls them. His saying "nénin" in reference to his mother's face, the point of a bare elbow, and a biscuit may mean that he perceives a commonality among these objects, but it does not mean that he fails to distinguish among them. The child has apparently conceived of a loose associative organization of certain aspects of experience which he tentatively represents with a familiar and similarly associative word.

The "nénin"-like words are usually reported as occurring among the first words that the child uses — sometime around the end of his first year. According to Piaget,[15] the child at this age has not yet achieved the notion of the constancy of objects — that is, the realization that objects exist and endure independent of himself and his actions. Until the child becomes aware of the permanence of objects, it would seem that he might well use a word to name individual, particular instances of perception or action: in the example used so far, each such instance was "nénin", but there was no OBJECT-NÉNIN.

Phase (B), the "fa fa" word stage, appears to begin midway into the second year and is the phenomenon that has been described over and over again as the child's learning the meaning of a word, by the process of 'generalizing to new instances': the child typically first uses the word in a restricted domain — particular flowers in a particular bowl — but very soon generalizes all of his experiences of the original instance (what he sees, smells, hears, feels) to other new instances which differ from one another but nevertheless remain within the same semantic field. Here the child does appear to have differentiated a particular class of objects (or events) on the basis of their perceptual and functional attributes, and this cognitive representation is the basis for his beginning to use the word. It is of considerable interest that this period coincides with the period in which the child achieves object constancy.

It is only after he has learned to represent classes of objects with

[15]   Jean Piaget, *The construction of reality in the child*, 1954.

particular word-forms in the last half of the second year that the second kind of over-inclusion occurs in Phase (C). The data are not altogether clear on this point but it does appear that the kind of over-inclusion involved when the child calls all four-legged animals "dog" or all fruits "apple" or all vehicles "truck" differs from the "nénin" over-inclusion in a fundamental way. Phase (C) involves words with overlapping semantic fields in adult meaning-reference. That is, all dogs are quadrupeds, all apples are fruits, and all trucks are vehicles, but not all quadrupeds are dogs, *etc.* The child probably has a conceptual representation of an OBJECT DOG, but it is probably not true that the representation also includes all of the perceptual features belonging to horses, cats, sheep, *etc.* It is not clear to what extent the child knows the differences among different quadrupeds, but he does appear to have learned a larger cognitive domain, only part of which has been semantically represented (as "dog"). It seems entirely reasonable to expect him to adopt a strategy in which he uses an available word-form as an aid in representing different but related objects.

Lewis has detailed the "expansion and contraction of meanings" in one child's reference to four-legged animals. The form "tee" occurred initially at 1 year, 9 months in reference to a cat and was extended subsequently to a small dog and then a cow. "Goggie" was introduced in reference to a toy dog and then replaced "tee" for referring to small dogs. "Tee" was then extended to horses, and after "hosh" replaced "tee", "hosh" was extended to large dogs. Finally, the child differentiated five forms at 2 years: "pushie" (for cats), "moo-ka", "hosh", "biggie-goggie", and "goggie" (for both small dogs and toy dogs). This progression occurred over a five-month period from 1 year, 9 months to 2 years[16]. However, Lewis reported that the meaning of "fa-fa" developed over the period from one year, four months to one year, 10 months.

It is important to note that both the first and the third of these stages include only a few examples from particular children. Children appear to use only one or two "nénin"-like words in the

[16]   M. M. Lewis, *Language, thought and personality*, 1963, 51.

beginning, and reports of over-inclusion of the type described as later (Phase C) typically include only a few examples, and these are impressively consistent across children — it seems that many children go through a period in which all four-legged animals are dogs, and all vehicles are trucks or choo-choos. It is almost as if the child were reasoning, "I know about dogs, that thing is not a dog, I don't know what to call it, but it is like a dog!"

One way to explain the fact that Allison did not persist in using many substantive words in the period from 9 to 17 months was that the use of such words was particular; she could not generalize to new instances and so continue the use of the word primarily because she had not yet realized object constancy. Where there was no conceptual representation of the object, the use of a word to refer to it could not endure.

Piaget has described the child's acquisition of "object concept" — the notion of the permanence and independence of objects when removed in space and time. The child learns that things exist, that they exist apart from himself, that they recur after he experiences their disappearance ("perceived displacements") and, finally, that they recur without his having perceived their disappearance ("the representation of displacements not perceived")[17]. Inasmuch as children are still progressing toward representation of objects in the first 18 months, it should not be surprising that reference to objects — the use of substantive word-forms — was not the dominant speech behavior observed with Allison in this period of time. Although different substantive words occurred, except for person names and names of very familiar objects, they were not among the most frequent words that she used, and many forms tended not to persist in use. Piaget described objects as inextricably bound to context and to the action schemas in which they are perceived. It would follow that the substantive words that do occur are also a part of such action schemas[18] but, further, if they cannot be used independently of such action and original context, then their drop from use

---

[17]   Jean Piaget, *The construction of reality in the child*, 1954, 102.
[18]   As Roger Brown has pointed out, in "*A first language*", in prep.

might be expected. The mortality of both the words "flower" and "dog" after Allison first used them can be explained in just this way. "Dog" was used in the country, where we live in the summer; it did not occur again after our return to the city. "Flower" was said by Allison during a week's stay in Florida; it did not occur again after our return home. Apparently, dogs and flowers in the city were new and different objects. In contrast, caretaker persons (Mommy, Daddy, and babysitter), certain foods, and favored toys virtually form a large portion of context — participating in indefinitely many action schemas — apparently explaining the persistence with which they continue after first use (in Allison's speech, and as reported by Guillaume and Leopold).

In the fifth stage (12 to 16 months) of the development of object concept, the child comes to an awareness of an object as "permanent individual substance" within his immediate spatial field, although he cannot take account of changes of position which affect the object outside the field of his direct perception. "There is therefore nothing surprising in the fact that the child of 12 to 16 months of age considers as objects only those images that are near, and remains doubtful with regard to bodies subjected to invisible displacements"[19]. The extent to which the WORDS that the child uses at this time are represented conceptually (that is, lexical representation) must, of necessity, be in a special kind of limbo — dependent upon the context of reference and the child's action with respect to referents. One cannot, then, speak of the child's acquiring 'features of meaning'. His representations of the meanings of words are not 'incomplete' with respect to the number of features or the differentiation of features, but, rather, the representation of MEANING waits upon the representation of the OBJECT — and, for all intents and purposes, the early meaning of the 'word' and the representation of the object may be isomorphic. Thus, the conclusion that substantive words have a strong 'word-image' cognitive representation.

The following three examples from the first three video tape

Jean Piaget, *The construction of reality in the child*, 1954, 87.

samples provided evidence of the change in Allison's use of substantive words relative to the action schemas in which they occurred:

I: 31 (16,3)
(A picking up doll)	ə wídə/
(A walking to truck with doll)	baby/ baby/
(A trying to put doll in truck)	ə wídə/
(A puts doll in truck)	
	there/

In this example, in the first sample, Allison said "baby" when she
was holding the doll. Although she evidently knew what she wanted
to do with the doll, she did not say "truck" in the sample, and I have
no record that she had said "truck" at the time, elsewhere. The baby
was her favorite doll; she had never seen the toy truck before.
Allison did not see the toy truck again until the second sample:

II: 35, 36, 37 (19,2)
(A sees truck on big chair; goes toward it)	
Oh, I see a truck.	
(A picks up truck; putting truck on floor)	baby/ baby/
(A puts truck down; looking around)	baby/ baby/
(A reaching for her bag)	baby/
(A looking into bag)	baby!/ baby!/
(A pulling doll out of bag)	baby!/
There's the baby.	
(A taking doll to truck on floor)	truck/
Truck.	
(A trying to sit doll in truck)	baby/

Allison remembered that particular truck in terms of her previous
experience with it: putting her doll into the truck three months
earlier. The word "truck" was frequently used elsewhere at this
time, and it occurred six times in this sample. However, Allison
did not say "truck" until after she had, in a sense, reestablished the

original situation (by bringing the doll to the truck), and it was the structure of the original situation that·was evidently most salient to her. She was not 'naming' the truck a baby; she clearly knew what relation the truck had to the baby. Neither was the word "baby" a simple associative response on seeing the truck. When she saw the truck, she acted upon it in the best way she knew — precisely as she had acted on it before, but with a critical difference. She no longer had the doll in hand (or in sight), but her perception of the doll, and the schema of the doll in the truck had evidently endured. Whereas at 16,3 she had operated on what was in the situation (the doll), at 19,2 she acted on an object (the doll) that was removed from the situation but evidently a part of her conceptual representation of the situation.

At the time of the third sample, Allison had not seen the truck since the previous video session, five weeks earlier:

III: 50, 51, 52, 53 (20,3)

(A reaching for truck on table)   truck/
    You take the truck and I'll bring you a
    little juice. Take the truck back to the
    chair.

                                                    brrm/
(A starts back with truck; puts it down;
picking it up)   wee/
(A goes to little chair, then to big chair,
then turning to floor)   sit/
(A puts truck down; standing up,
looking around, excited)   baby doll/ baby doll/
(M pointing to doll)
    There she is. There's the baby doll.
(A laughs; running to doll on floor)   running/ running/
    Running.
(A picks up doll; running back to truck
with it)   Allison/ baby doll/
                                                    truck/

    Baby doll truck.

(A sitting doll in truck)   sit/ sit/
(A starts to move truck)

                                      up/ town/
Uptown?

                                      bye/

Allison immediately named the truck on seeing it again. Her two subsequent utterances "brrm" and "wee" made reference to trucks in general. This truck apparently was now perceived relative to her summary representation of an OBJECT-TRUCK, but it was still a particular truck tied to the structure of a particular situation, as her subsequent utterances rather eloquently demonstrated.

This account of the dependence of the representation of lexical meaning of substantive words on the child's development of object constancy would appear to explain, at least in part, three phenomena that are reported over and over again in the language development literature: (1) the phenomenon of over-inclusion, (2) the mortality of words in use in the first half of the second year, and (3) the sudden increase in 'naming' behavior in the second half of the second year. The conceptual representation of objects and the lexical representation of words appear to occur together. Where there was no representation of the object, there was over-inclusion in the use of particular words or the use of words in only specific contexts. The tokens of each word that occurred were not unified — each occurred as a separate instance of an object in a particular context or action.

The great increase in the number of different substantive words in Allison's speech occurred at approximately 17 months — the same increase in 'naming' in the last half of the second year has been reported with great frequency in the literature. All of the uses of single words discussed so far have one thing in common — they are used by children to make reference to objects which have criterial features for reference which are seen, heard, felt, or otherwise PERCEIVED (or USED in particular ways). Thus, although there are 'errors' of under-inclusion and over-inclusion, children in their second year categorize certain perceptual phenomena and use word-forms to make reference to classes of objects.

Other single words that children use — including "more", "no", "gone", "away", "up", "off", "there", "stop", — do not have the same potential for independent 'word-image' representation. Such words are inherently relational terms — FUNCTION words — which make reference to aspects of behavior that extend across classes of objects and events, and are dependent on other referents in behavior and context for making reference. Thus, objects and events which differ perceptually and functionally from one another, nevertheless share certain behaviors, that is, they exist, cease to exist, and recur, and they are acted upon in similar ways.

Moreover, the words "more", "there", and "away" occurred in two-word utterances in Allison's speech from the age of 14 months. One or two such utterances usually occurred each day; there were thirteen utterances longer than a single word recorded on the video tape at 16,3, and these are presented in Table 2, p. 42. Because such words as these cannot make reference without the support of context, and because of their inherently relational nature, one might expect them to occur among the earliest syntactic utterances when children begin to use grammar. That such function words occur among the earliest syntactic utterances in early grammar has been reported frequently[20]. They also occur as single-word utterances before syntax, and, in Allison's speech, they were the most frequently used words. Their occasional occurrence in two-word utterances during the pre-syntax stage of single-word utterances should not be surprising.

4.3. THE USE OF FUNCTION FORMS AS SINGLE-WORD UTTERANCES

A relatively small group of words have been identified as function forms on the basis of their frequency, endurance, and referential

---

[20] See Martin D. S. Braine, "The ontogeny of English phrase structure", 1963; Wick Miller and Susan Ervin, "The development of grammar in child language", 1964; Lois Bloom, *Language development*, 1970; and Roger Brown, "*A first language*", in prep.

function in Allison's speech: "more", "there", "up", "uh oh", "away", "gone", "no", and "stop". Not only did these words occur frequently and persistently in the period from 9 to 20 months, but they were each used in situations which shared features of behavior and context.

4.3.1. The Use of "more"

There is no record of how or how often "more" was used in the speech that Allison heard from infancy on. However, there was one situation in which "more" was used with a conscious awareness on my part — during meals, after Allison had finished a food, and she was offered additional food either with the comment "here's more (meat, milk, juice, etc.)", or with a question, "do you want more (meat, milk, etc.)?". Further, the word "more" was usually emphasized. The use of "more" in a comment or question having to do with the recurrence or additional instances of events outside of food and meals was also possible, for example, "let's read some more". However, there was not the same conscious awareness of the use of "more" in such contexts, and, in any event, there was not the same deliberate emphasis on the form "more".

There was no behavioral evidence for determining comprehension of "more". If Allison was asked "do you want more cheese?" (or whatever she had just eaten), she looked at or looked for the CHEESE. If simply asked "do you want more?", she looked at or looked for the cheese (or whatever she had just eaten), that is, if she did indeed want more. There was no direct referent for "more" that was not also the referent for some other element of the utterance in the context.

From 12 to 13 months, Allison used the word "again" on three occasions: once as a comment on her having torn the stem from a paper flower AGAIN, and twice as a request for a book to be read to her AGAIN just after it was read the first time. The word "again" did not reappear in her speech until the end of her second year.

Allison first said "more" when she was 16 months, 2 days old. She used the word to REQUEST foods and drink after eating or drinking initial portions. Thus, she had food, ate it, and requested the recurrence of food — or "more" food. Within two days, she extended the use of the word to a totally different situation — lying on her dressing table, she said "more" to REQUEST her baby sitter to tickle her again, after she had just tickled her. Thereafter, she said "more" to request the recurrence of such events as reading another book, playing Ring-a-Rosy again, sliding on her slide again, wearing the same coverall she had worn in the morning, *etc.* She continued to request the recurrence of objects (including food and drink) after such objects had existed and had ceased to exist or been depleted. There were only occasional instances of "more" as a general request form — without previous existence or occurrence — in the period from 16 to 20 months.

Several weeks later, at 16 months, 3 weeks, Allison was playing with a scrap of fabric; she saw another piece of the fabric on the sofa, and went after it, saying "more". This was the first recorded instance of "more" used as a COMMENT on another instance of an object (see also I: 75 "more cow" also at 16,3). This use of "more" was frequent thereafter — for example, Allison said "more" as she watched me make a 'cuff' on her sleeve after I had made a cuff on her other sleeve, when she saw other instances of cookies, blocks, shoes and other objects.

The use of "more" in situations in which the recurrence or another instance of an object or event was the focus is the same use of the word reported in the earlier syntax study[21], when the word occurred alone and in syntactic contexts (with both noun and verb forms) in the speech of three other children. In an independent analysis of the same data (from two of the children in the syntax study), Weiner reported that "more" was not used by Kathryn or Gia to request additional instances of something that still existed (that is, without intervening depletion or nonexistence). However, Kathryn and Gia both used "more" to REQUEST addition to something that they had, in the later unpublished data[22]. There is no record of

[21] Lois Bloom, *Language development*, 1970.
[22] Susan Weiner, "'More' and 'Less'; The study of a comparative dimension", 1971.

Allison's using "more" in this additional sense — to request other instances of something she still had.

The use of "more" to signal RECURRENCE or ANOTHER INSTANCE OF can be schematized (for the pre-syntax data from Allison and for the early syntactic speech of Kathryn, Eric and Gia) as follows:

(a) $X \rightarrow \emptyset$; $X' = more$, that is, X exists, ceases to exist, and a new instance (or X itself) recurs and is "more".

(b) X; $X' = more$, that is, X exists, and another instance of X occurs (or is noticed, picked up, *etc.*) and is "more".

The comparative was not used:

(c) X, X', $X + X' = more$ (than X), that is, where X and X' together result in a greater quantity than original X, and X and X' together are "more".

4.3.2. The Use of "there", "uh oh", and "up"

The form "uh oh" was first used at 14 months; "there" was first used at 15 months, 1 week and its early use was in response to the question "Where's X?" Both forms endured throughout the single-word utterance period. From 13 to 14 months, Allison said [ə↑], often when pointing to objects, but this form no longer occurred after 14 months and it seemed to have been replaced by "there". "There" and "uh oh" functioned to point out objects or people that were noticed or found (with or without gesture). "Uh oh" often commented on events that were, more often than not, sudden or somewhat startling. The use of "there" was not mutually exclusive with the use of "more" — that is, "there" was used at times to point out another instance of or the recurrence of some object, and the following speech event was recorded at age 17 months, 1 week:

(8)   (M making batter for cookies,
        shows A sugar on batter before
        beating it in each time. M adding

sugar into bowl; A can no
longer see into bowl; straining
to see the batter)   more/ more/
(M showing her the batter in the
bowl)   there more!/

The word "up" was first used by Allison as a REQUEST to be taken out of her high chair (which involved picking her up). Within a few days after initial use, Allison commented "up" when she got up or climbed up herself, when other people got up, when she picked up objects or pulled people up. The word "up" was the second most frequent form used in the video tape sample at 16,3 most often said as she climbed up onto the big chair.

Allison used "up" frequently in both comment and request situations that involved different people, objects and events in the action UP. The range of situations in which "up" was used was virtually identical to the states of affairs accompanying 'up' described by Leopold. For example, "One evening [at approximately 16,2] she [Hildegard] said often and with enjoyment 'up', when she wanted to get up on the davenport."[23] This is the situation video-recorded at 16,3 as Allison repeatedly climbed up on the big chair, saying "up" (see the Appendix). Allison also used "up" as a comment on a stative relation but far less frequently, for example, pointing to a toy on a high shelf. Leopold also reported "'up' was frequently used ... both for a condition at rest ... and for an upward motion ... [for example, at 21 months] looking at candy on the mantel, she said 'way up'." Both Allison and Leopold's Hildegard used "up" as a REQUEST form before using it as a COMMENT.

Allison did not begin to use the contrasting form "down" until two months after she began to use "up". Both were generally used appropriately with respect to the direction of action or the location of the object relative to Allison. However, the use of "down" in the video sample at 16,3 indicated some ambiguity that could be traced to ambiguous uses of the terms "up" and "down" in the adult

[23]   Werner Leopold, *Speech development of a bilingual child*, Vol. 1, 1939, 35-36.

model, for example, "sit up" and "sit down" in the same situations. Approximately one half of the occurrences of "up" and "down" in the sample referred to Allison's movements, Allison either getting up or sitting down. Aside from two uninterpretable instances of "up", its use was appropriate. However, there were several ambiguous instances of "down", for example:

I: 63 (16,3)
(A tries to get on chair; then walks to
other side of Mommy; trying to make M
get off the chair)   down/ down/ up/
   Down?

                                           up/up/
   Up? Mommy off that chair?
(M stands up; A trying to get up onto
chair)   down/
(A gets on chair; sits)   up// baby/

Leopold reported that apparently for a short time after its initial use, "'up' was used also for the opposite wish — *down* being said only upon request. This does not mean that the directional sense of 'up' was not well understood; the use of a word in the opposite sense is frequent in child language, and several examples of this phenomenon were observed in Hildegard's speech."[24]

4.3.3. *The Use of "away", "a'gone", "no", and "stop"*

Thus far it has been reported that Allison began to comment on or point out the EXISTENCE of objects, people, and events (first using "uh oh" and "there" at 14 and 15 months). The use of "more", initially as a request and subsequently as a comment was first reported at 16 months and it was used thereafter in situations that were distinguished by the RECURRENCE or another instance of an object or event. Before her first birthday, however, Allison had begun to talk about the disappearance of objects, people and events.

[24] Werner Leopold, *Speech development of a bilingual child*, Vol. 1, 1939, 36.

Allison's earliest words, from 9 to 10 months were "Da" (alternating with [dǽi]), "Ma", "car", and "cat" (the use of these words is discussed in 4.4. below). At 10 months of age she began to use "away" with the clear intent of a direction or request — to do away with or throw away some object such as a stone or a piece of dirt. Allison would pick up the object, saying "away" with a directive gesture — for example, towards the kitchen where the trash was kept indoors, or out of the sand box on the playground. This was essentially the way in which the word had been presented to her — whenever she put a stone or dirt to her mouth, I would take it, make an appropriate grimace and say something like "let's throw it away". Within three days, Allison began to use "away" to comment on the disappearance of objects and people, for example, "away" just after Daddy left in the morning; "away" just after an airplane she had been watching disappeared from the sky, *etc.* Thereafter, Allison began to say "away" as an accompaniment to waving 'bye bye'. At 14 months, Allison was taught "a'gone" (all gone) by her baby sitter in reference to her finishing all of her food or drink, a situation in which she had previously said "away". Thereafter, "away" and "a'gone" were used in the same kinds of situations (although "away" was no longer used at mealtimes as formerly) — to comment on disappearance, or the nonexistence of an object or person just after its immediate presence in the context.

From 11 to 14 months, Allison would vehemently protest unwanted events by saying something like "nə nə nə nə nə" with appropriate gesture and emphasis — for example, when another child took her toy, when she didn't want to wear a particular dress, when she didn't want her diaper changed, a bath, etc. At about 14 months, Allison began to articulate "no" in these situations as an expression of protest or REJECTION. At the same time, she would also look at or touch forbidden areas or objects such as electric wires, plants, and adult books and records and say "no", as in the following example from the video tape at 16,3[25]:

[25]   See, also, events I: 4 and 69 (16,3) in the Appendix for examples of Allison's use of 'prohibitive' "no" in such a situation. René Spitz (*The first year of life*, 1965) described the development of this sense of negation as the "first semantic

I: 46 (16,3)
(M moves microphone, A turns, touching
microphone)   no/
(A puts book down, reaches for
microphone)
   No.
(A cries)
(M pushes microphone back)
   Well, I'm sorry. Can't play with the
   microphone.
(A touches microphone)
                        no/
(A spanking own hands)   no no/
   No. No no. No no.

Just before she was 15 months, Allison began to say "no" in the following situations: holding a book with a bunny on the cover, she turned the book over and looking at the blank cover said "no, no". This same behavior was repeated with the picture of a baby on the Pampers box, pictures on cereal boxes, cans, juice cartons, photographs in frames, *etc.* Often Allison would look at the picture of the baby, say "baby", turn the photograph around, look at the blank side and say "no, no", as in the following example:

I: 37 (16,3)
(A holding picture out to photographer's
assistant, off camera)   there/
   Are you showing it to her?
(A puts picture down)
                        down/

---

symbol" or "gesture" in the child's development. However, Allison used this prohibitive sense of "no" only in situations similar to those in which it had been presented to her. The examples in the sample at 16,3 all relate to the wire attached to a microphone. Other kinds of negation were far more productive in her behavior, that is, comments on disappearance or nonexistence, and expressions of rejection or protest.

Where's the girl?

girl/

Girl.

(A turns picture over so she can't see the
girl)

no/

(A turning it back to picture side)   there/

(A turns it so she can't see girl)

no wídə/

No, there's no picture back there, is it?

girl/

Where's the girl?

(A turns it back to picture side)

there/ ---/ there/

She also began to say "no" as she looked into any container such
as a shopping bag or box and found it empty. This last use of "no",
to comment on NONEXISTENCE where existence of something was
somehow expected, endured — along with the more frequent use
of "no" to express REJECTION — and its use was in contrast with the
use of "away" and "a'gone" as described previously in situations of
DISAPPEARANCE, or the nonexistence of objects or persons that had
existed in the context just previously.

Allison used "stop" from 13 months in situations where some
ongoing event ceased, for example, when music ended on her
phonograph, when the car stopped, when the food blender was
turned off, etc. "Stop" always occurred as a comment on CESSATION;
there was no record of Allison's using the word as a request or
direction.

Thus, there seemed to be a strong tendency for Allison to talk
about objects, persons and events which ceased to exist in the
context or which did not exist in a context where existence was
somehow expected. The evidence of this tendency to comment on
nonexistence, disappearance, and cessation was the use of certain
word-forms in particular situations that shared features of behavior
and context. The forms so far described — "away", "a'gone", "no",

and "stop" — occurred frequently and continued to be used throughout the single-word utterance period. Other, similar kinds of words also occurred from time to time — usually in a specific reference or context. For example, Allison learned "nudie" after some confusion, thinking at first that it was her belly and/or her navel. However, she eventually used the word in reference to her bare self, but also to any exposed skin — for example, her arm after taking off a sweater. On one occasion she pointed to a dowel after she had removed all of the stacking rings and exclaimed "nudie!"

It was clear then that Allison talked about objects, persons, and events in their absence — what is not clear is whether the speech events in which the words "away", "a'gone", "no", "stop", "nudie", *etc.* occurred were the only kinds of speech events in which she did talk about nonexistence. That is, it is reasonable to assume that children look for misplaced objects and utter the names of the objects while doing so; certainly children call for "Mommy" when they know Mommy is gone. In any study of the use of speech, one is limited to an analysis of the actual words that occur and the context and behavior in the speech events in which the words are heard. It is more difficult to study naturalistic contexts alone, to see what children say in specific situations, than to study only those situations in which particular word-forms occur. However, it would be nice to know all of the kinds of utterances that were used by a child in particular kinds of speech events. For example, it might have been the case that Allison was as likely to say "blender" or "noise" as to say "stop" when the blender stopped, or as likely to say "plane" as to say "away" when it had passed over. I do not think so. Allison occasionally used the names of objects and people to comment on some aspect of their function in the context or, when the referents did not exist in the context, to report something about them WITHOUT EXPECTATION OF THEIR EXISTENCE IN THE IMMEDIATE SPEECH EVENT. For example, when at the dinner table, Allison said "playground" it was certainly possible that she was commenting on the fact that there was no playground in the dining room. However, because there was no evidence of a reasonable expectation on Allison's part of a playground in the dining room, and because Allison had been to the playground during the day, it seems more reasonable to interpret her utterance as a REPORT about her visit to the playground and not as a comment on its nonexistence in the dining room. She certainly did not look for a playground in the dining room.

McNeill has discussed essentially this phenomenon: the occurrence of a word in the absence of a direct referent. He reports two instances in which a child said a word in situations where the child's assertion was not true, although it would have been true in a similar situation at a different time. In one instance the child said "hot" after touching an empty coffee cup; in the second instance the child said "'nana" when looking at the top of the refrigerator. Coffee cups are usually hot; bananas were usually on that particular refrigerator[26]. However, McNeill did not interpret these two utterances as expressions of the nonexistence of 'hotness' or bananas. The interpretation that was offered was that the child had used a single-word utterance to express a GRAMMATICAL relation — the attribution of properties when she said "hot" and the locative relation when she said "'nana". To be sure, one cannot know the full semantic meaning of any utterance of any child — and so it would be nice to have many more examples such as these before inferring what the child might have intended by the utterances when she said them. There are at least two other plausible explanations for their occurrence however. To begin with, there is a strong tradition that describes the meanings of words in terms of the associations somehow linked with them. Clearly, "hot" and "'nana" in the above speech events have strong associations with aspects of the context in which the words occurred. Further, McNeill did not report whether the child had been known to use the words "cup", "coffee", or "refrigerator". If she did not 'know' such words then the words "hot" and "'nana" might have been all that she was able to say in those situations, and the associations the words had were strong enough for the utterances to be appropriate.

---

[26] David McNeill, *The acquisition of language*, 1970, 24, 32.

It was clear that Allison used the forms "more", "there", "away", "stop" to talk about objects, persons, and events that she had never 'named' — and would not 'name' for many more months. She had never said such words as "blender", "lunch", "tickle", *etc.* Substantive words occurred, to be sure, and these are discussed in the next section. But Allison was able to talk about certain notions like existence, nonexistence, disappearance, cessation and recurrence in relation to many more referents than she presumably had specific labels for.

However, there is no record of the extent to which Allison intended the same notions existence, nonexistence, and recurrence by her use of such words as "hat", "ball", "tumble", *etc.* In an effort to correlate the form of utterances with their inferred function, it is safer to draw inferences about the use of a particular form that recurs with consistency in speech events that have features of behavior and context in common — such as the use of "more" in situations of recurrence. When radically different forms are used in recurring contexts, inferences about underlying function or intent can be made with far less confidence. That is, it is not at all clear that "hat", "ball", and "cookie" are comments on nonexistence in situations where each has disappeared; the idea that they represent requests for recurrence might be equally plausible in many instances. The potential for ambiguity is greater. It is also true that the use of a constant form in repeated contexts 'triggers' the interpretation on the part of the investigator. But it does not necessarily follow that the use of the form is the only possible behavior or speech available to the child. For the study of the extent to which children do talk about such notions as existence, nonexistence, and recurrence to be complete, it would be best to be able to describe all of the child's different behaviors in these particular situations in his experience. It was doubtful that Allison used the above words every time the particular contexts occurred for her.

In summary, Allison used certain constant forms in repeated contexts and it was reasonable to conclude that her use of these forms was coherent. Moreover, there have been other reports of similar forms in the pre-syntax speech described by others.

Leopold's description of Hildegard's use of "up" has already been discussed; he also discussed "mehr" as one of the more frequent words in her speech and "the only German word which ... survived in active use ... throughout the period in which English was predominant". He described the use of "'alle' ... in the meaning of [both] 'gone', [and] 'empty' [as] one of her most frequent words from [1 year, 7 months] to [2 years] and beyond". Hildegard used both "no" and "nein" in apparent expression of rejection; "no" came to be the preferred form "with the meanings 'I do not want to', 'I am not allowed to', and 'it is not so'"[27].

Guillaume discussed "le langage de volonté ... c'est-à-dire l'élément verbal des réactions de négation (refus de soins, d'objets, aversion de certains actes ou traitements) et des réactions positives de désir (désir d'un objet, d'un acte, de sa continuation ou de son renouvellement)"[28] in the second year.

4.4. THE USE OF SUBSTANTIVE FORMS AS SINGLE-WORD UTTERANCES

The functions of other words that Allison used could be described with less confidence. To begin with, except for "Mommy", "Dada", "Mimi", and "Baby" the substantive forms she used each occurred less frequently. It was possible to infer, in most situations, what it

[27] Werner Leopold, *Speech development of a bilingual child*, Vol. 1, 1939, 104-105; 109; 34-35; 109-114.
[28] "the language of the will ... that is, the verbal element in reactions of negation (rejection of caretaking, of objects, aversion to certain activities or attentions) and positive reactions of desire (desire for an object, an action, its continuation or recurrence)". Guillaume reported examples from as early as 12 to 13 months. Interestingly, the examples are utterances with more than one morpheme even at that age, and the earliest examples are negative markers in juxtaposition with another word. The other examples (also more than one word long) include expressions of fear, pain and recurrence. "Encore" ('more' or 'again') is the only one of these words mentioned with the age it appeared (14,3 days). Guillaume implied that "non" occurred alone because he mentioned that it did not occur in juxtaposition with other words. The negative marker used in juxtaposition came from the adult "Il n'y a pas" or "Il n'y a plus". Paul Guillaume, "Les débuts de la phrase dans le langage de l'enfant", 1927.

was she was talking about when Allison used different substantive forms, but specific functions of particular words were potentially ambiguous more often than not. For example, at 14 months, Allison and I were walking in the early evening and Allison looked up from her stroller at the moon. She said "moon", and several minutes later, "Mimi". Her babysitter (Mimi) had pointed out the moon to her on other walks and I interpreted these two utterances as somehow making reference to such an association between the moon and Mimi. What was the function of "moon" — was the word used simply to name it, or to point it out, or, was "moon" somehow inextricably bound up with Mimi in Allison's mind when she said it? Further along in that same walk in the evening, Allison continued to watch the moon, and the words "moon", "Mimi", and "Mama" occurred often as we moved along and stopped at each intersection. At one intersection, Allison looked up at the moon from her stroller and said "stop". That night at the dinner table she reported the events of the walk to her father, and she used the words "moon", "Mimi", and "Mama" several times. After several minutes she said, quite clearly, "moon stop". It seemed that Allison had not differentiated the movement of her stroller from her perception of the movement of the moon — the moon did indeed 'stop' at those intersections. But little can be said about the function of the utterance "moon". It was there, Mama was there, it had been there when Mimi was there, and it had 'stopped'. Allison's use of "moon" somehow made reference to all of these experiences, but whether or not she perceived the "moon" as actor or object was unknowable. With most such words, there were always alternative interpretations of how they were used — as discussed previously with the utterances "hot" and "'nana" reported by McNeill.

However, it was possible to say something more about Allison's use of words that named people — "Mama", "Dada", "Mimi", and "Baby" (in reference to herself). From their first appearance at nine or ten months, until approximately 16 months, these words appeared to be used in three ways. Most often, Allison would comment "Mama" or "Dada" as if pointing out or naming Mama to another person or persons. These utterances frequently seemed to 'announce'

Mama, Dada, or Mimi, particularly when Mama, Dada, or Mimi entered the scene. A second use of these person names was as a 'greeting' — Allison would run into a room, exclaiming "Dada!" Both comments and greetings could be interpreted as simply naming — attaching a linguistic sign or label to the perceived event of Mama, Dada, or Mimi. During this time, Allison used such words as vocatives — to call for someone — but this was less frequent.

At 16 months, Allison began to point out objects that belonged to or were somehow associated with Mama, Dada, or Mimi. For example, she said "Mama" when she looked at, touched, or pointed to my lunch, my gloves, or my dress; she said "Dada" when she took notice of his bathrobe, his briefcase, and the bottles of gin and vermouth on the kitchen counter. However, such objects as these that were associated with or that belonged to Mama, Dada, or Mimi were objects that Allison had never named directly. That is, there was no record of her ever using the words "lunch", "glove", "dress", "briefcase", or "martini". Persons were associated with particular objects, and Allison was able to talk about such objects, to make reference to them, by using person names in such contexts.

What evidence would have led to the conclusion that Allison, indeed, intended a more explicit relational notion — such as agent-of-possession? If Allison had said either "Dada" or "briefcase" at one time or another — if there were evidence that both forms were somehow available and used in similar states of affairs as when Allison saw Daddy's briefcase, then one might want to conclude that the use of the person name was motivated in such situations by Allison's awareness of the relation between person and object. If so, then the variation in the form of the utterance in similar contexts might reflect differences in semantic intent: the one form "briefcase" being the name of the object; the other form "Dada" being the name of the person who used it, owned it, put it there, or was otherwise associated with or related to it. Such evidence did occur two months later, in the use of successive single-word utterances already discussed. However, the use of person names at 16 months in reference to associated objects — that were not also named — appeared to be early evidence of a primitive notion that included both persons and objects in an as yet nonspecific relation[29].

Subsequently, shortly before she was 17 months old, Allison began to use the words "Mama", "Dada", "Mimi", and "Baby" in situations in which it appeared that Mama, Dada, Mimi or herself was the actor of an intended or imminent action. For example, Allison said "Mama" when she was unable to open a door and she stood aside to let me open it; or when her doll carriage was stuck and she turned to me for help in freeing it; "Dada" as she brought something to Daddy to fix; and quite often, "Baby" when she reached for something she wanted to do like open a package, peek through a door, take the mail from the mailbox, *etc*. Again, these events most often involved actions that Allison had not named. Whether she 'knew' such words in the sense of understanding them or not, Allison did not SAY "open", "fix", "look", "take out", *etc*.

However, it was also the case that such use of person names during an ongoing or imminent action or event was ambiguous. If Dada was fixing, or reading, or walking, or pushing, *etc*., Allison's saying "Dada" could not be distinguished as Dada the person, Dada the doer, or Dada located. When she reached out for a package that Mama was opening, there was little doubt that she wanted to do the opening. BUT, her utterance "Baby" in such a situation could have represented the desired location for the package (in Allison's hands), the goal of Mama's action (giving to Allison) as well as the desired agency of an action (Allison opening), *etc*. It seems that once committed to attributing function to such utterances, there are always alternative possibilities, and the evidence in such situations could not distinguish among the possibilities. Allison referred to events with Mama, Dada, Mimi or herself as object of an action less often: examples included saying "Mama" as she closed the kitchen door with Mama in the kitchen; saying "Baby" as she held out her arms to be picked up. Again, there was no way to distinguish among possible alternative functions, for example, location of Mama or Baby.

---

[29]   Oscar Bloch ("Premiers stades du langage de l'enfant", 1921) also described his children's referring to objects by naming the person associated with them.

It appeared then, that reference to the earliest primitive notions of persons in relation to objects, actions, and locations derived from the use of person names in associative reference to objects and events that Allison apparently had no other words for. It is possible that the MEANING of the word "Daddy" was extended or enlarged to include phenomena such as objects associated with Daddy, or events in which Daddy acted. Certain objects associated with Daddy or events in which Daddy acted were somehow perceived only in terms of Daddy, as Allison organized her experience of objects and persons in her environment, and could not otherwise be coded than with the word "Daddy". That is, her perception of different objects, and her activity with respect to such objects, led her to the realization that there were domains for certain objects that were different from one another, and yet similar in that they were used by, worn by, sat on, *etc.*, by certain people. It is certainly the case that such objects and events are so 'named' for the child — children hear "that's Daddy's" and "Daddy does it" in reference to things that belong to Daddy and things that Daddy does.

This account of the child somehow categorizing certain phenomena and using person names to 'label' them, is somewhat analogous to the description of the use of such early words as "nénin", and, indeed, several of the diary studies report the early FIRST use of person names to refer to objects and locations associated with certain people (Guillaume's account, for example). However, there were two important differences at this later point in development. First, Allison had hit on an association that was recognized by the adults around her and responded to accordingly. It is not difficult to imagine the most likely response from an adult to Allison's utterance "Daddy" as she pointed to Daddy's briefcase. No one told her "No, that's not Daddy, it's a briefcase"; but someone was usually quick to tell her "Yes, that's DADDY'S BRIEFCASE." But, more important, Allison was beginning to come to terms with the constancy and endurance of objects (achieving the notion of object permanence as described by Piaget), and her cognitive activity involved organizing objects according to the schemas in which they were perceived. There were objects which intersected with people whose names she knew. Recognizing such objects in relation to such schemas, she could use person names to refer to them.

Children experience intersecting phenomena and hear different messages that overlap to a considerable degree, that is, different utterances repeat certain words. Words like "Daddy" and "Mommy" occur in other, adult utterances in reference to different objects and events. It is only when the child begins to distinguish and mentally represent objects independently of their originally perceived schemas — that is, with the realization that bathrobes and briefcases are representable classes of objects which may or may not be 'of Daddy' — that the different relational categories linking persons and objects begin to be realized.

At about 17 months Allison began to use many more substantive words that referred to objects and events. There was a preponder-

TABLE 5

Most Frequent Forms That Were Not Noun Forms in the Model Language*: Allison from 17 to about 20 months

Form	Contexts
tumble	when anything fell spontaneously — either Allison, people, or objects
back	(a) when anything (such as Allison either walking or on her trike or playhorse) moved backwards (b) in the sense of coming back — most often when Allison pretended to go somewhere and then ran back (c) putting things back
catch	(a) when Allison threw a ball (with or without an intended receiver) (b) when Allison ran away and wanted to be chased
tire'	(a) when Allison pretended to sleep (b) when she saw someone either lying down or with eyes closed
turn	(a) when Allison turned, e.g. dancing (b) when Allison turned a lid, a cap or a toy

*   The forms here are in addition to those discussed in the text, for example, "there," "up," "no," etc.

ance of noun forms and, very often, such words appeared to occur with no other function than to name or point out objects or persons. This observation corresponds to the frequent report in the literature of the sudden increase in vocabulary in the second half of the second year, usually described as an increase in naming behavior.

There were other forms used from 17 months on that were not noun forms in the adult model language. The most frequent of these are presented in Table 5 along with a description of the contexts in which they occurred. Other such 'action' or 'event' words included "dance", "jump", "scream", "squeeze", "hug", "kiss", "go", (usually after cessation), "scrub", "bump", "carry", "kick", "cough", "shake", and "stir". By 19 months Allison had used five contrasting pairs of words with each member of the pair used at least five times, in relevant nonlinguistic contexts: *up*-*down, open*-*close, big*-*small, cold*-*hot, dirty*-*clean*. The starred words were those that were recorded as the first of the pair to be used with consistency.

Table 6 presents all of the words recorded on the video tape at 19,2. When these words and their relative frequencies of occurrence are compared with the words recorded at 16,3 (in Table 4), the difference in Allison's use of single-word utterances at the two different times is apparent. Although she was still saying only one word at a time, there were several important changes in the words that she used and the ways in which she used them in the course of three months from 16 to 19 months. She was evidently using different kinds of words and talking about different kinds of phenomena.

There were more different words in the second sample at 19,2 (62 different words) than in the first sample at 16,3 (30 different words), but individual words in the first sample occurred far more frequently than did the words in the second sample[30]. That is, Allison used many more different words but she used each word less often in the second sample than in the first. In the first sample, 7 of the 30 different words occurred 19 times or more; in the second

[30]   Numbers of different words include words occurring in multi-word utterances, not presented in Tables 4 and 6.

TABLE 6

Single-Word Utterances and their Frequency of Occurrence
Allison at 19 months, 2 weeks

Allison, 1	help, 2	step, 1
baby, 36	home, 9	there, 21
back, 4	horse, 4	towel, 1
bag, 1	juice, 6	truck, 6
bath, 5	knee, 1	tumble, 5
big, 5	man, 15	uh, 2
blanket, 3	Mary, 10	uh oh, 7
bop, 3	mmn, 3	up, 12
bowwow (wow), 4	Mommy, 29	
box, 4	moo, 7	
brrm, 3	more, 7	
burp, 1	no, 23	
chair, 5	nudie [nunu], 2	
clean, 1	off, 2	
cookie, 5	office, 1	
cover, 3	on, 1	
cow, 1	open, 1	
cup, 1	out, 3	
Daddy, 3	over there, 2	
dirty (da), 3	pig, piggy, 7	Most Frequent: baby, 36
down, 15	please, 1	Mommy, 29
duck, 2	Pop-Pop, 2	no, 23
gone, 1	scrub, 2	there, 21
hand, 2	small, 4	down, 15
head, 3	splash, 1	man, 15

sample, 4 of the 62 different words occurred 20 times or more. Also, in the first sample, 73% of the words occurred fewer than 10 times, whereas 87% of the words in the second sample occurred fewer than 10 times. Three of the most frequent words in the first sample: "more", (24 instances), "gone", (19 instances), and "up", (27 instances), occurred far less frequently in the second sample: "more", (7 instances), "gone", (1 instance), and "up", (12 instances). This trend toward the use of a greater number of words, each occurring less often, was progressive; 97 different words occurred as single words, and only 3 of these occurred more than 15 times at 20,3 (see Table 7).

The differences in the use of speech in each of the first three samples can be seen most readily when utterances in similar speech events are compared at each time. Following is a comparison of the use of single-word utterances during a snack of juice and cookies at 16, 3 with nearly the same situation at 19, 2, and again at 20, 3. The setting for these events was the same; the television studio at Teachers College, Allison, Mommy, a bag of 5 or 6 cookies, several paper cups, and a can of apple juice. The difference among the speech events at the three different times is essentially in how Allison talked about what she did. Almost all of her utterances accompanied a specific action by Allison on objects that were present

TABLE 7

Single-Word Utterances and their Frequency of Occurrence
Allison at 20 months, 3 weeks

again, 1	doll, 5	moo, 1	skip, 2	
ah, 2	down, 1	more, 13	snack, 2	
all gone, 1	drive, 1	napkin, 3	sneeze, 1	
Allison, 12	floor, 2	neck, 3	spill, 1	
away, 4	floppy, 1	no, 20	table, 2	
ba-back, 1	funny, 1	nose, 1	talk, 1	
ba-black, 1	glass, 5	nudie, 1	there, 3	
baby, 20	hair, 2	oh, 2	touch, 1	
back, 3	hand, 1	on, 9	towel, 1	
bag, 4	hat, 1	open, 1	town, 4	
bath, 1	hello, 1	out, 1	toy, 2	
Bloom, 2	help, 2	pat, 1	truck, 4	
boom, 1	here, 1	play, 2	tumble, 2	
box, 1	hi, 6	pin, 4	uh oh, 4	
bye, 1	home, 4	police, 1	up, 11	
car, 3	horse, 4	puppet, 10	walk, 1	
chair, 4	juice, 2	rain, 1	wee, 4	
clean, 6	lamb, 1	rest, 1	wipe, 1	Most Frequent:
coming, 3	lie down, 5	ride, 3	wiping, 7	Mommy, 23
cookie, 2	man, 2	rug, 1	wool, 1	baby, 20
cow, 7	mess, 1	running, 1	yummy, 4	no, 20
cup, 5	mike, 3	school, 3	zip, 4	
diaper, 11	mm, 8	scrub, 1		
dirt, 1	mm hm, 1	sharp, 1		
dirty, 5	Mommy, 23	sit, 6		

in the situation. In each of the events her actions had to do with the juice, cups, cookies, Allison, and Mommy. However, the words that she used differed, apparently because she seemed to be talking about the INTERACTION between the juice, cups, cookies, Allison, and Mommy at 19,2 and again at 20,3 but NOT at 16,3:

I: 14, 18, 19 (16,3)
   What's Mommy have? (M holding
   cookies)
(A reaching for cookie)   cookie/
   Cookie! O.K. Here's a cookie for you.
(A takes cookie; reaching with other hand
towards others in bag)   more/
   There's more in here. We'll have it in a
   little while.
(A picking up bag of cookies)   bag/
(A taking cookie M is holding)   cookie/
   Cookie. Hm, I think you're a hungry
   girl.
(A picking up empty cup and turning it
over)   uh uh uh oh/
(A puts cup down; reaching for more
juice)   more/
   More juice?
(M pours juice; A drinks juice, looks into
empty cup, squashes cup)
   Where's the juice?
(A gesturing 'gone')   gone/
   Gone.
   I think Mommy will have some juice.
(M pours self juice)
(A picking up empty cup)   more/
(A putting her cup aside)   more/
(A reaching for M's cup)   ə wídə/
   I'll give you some more. Here. I'll give
   you more.

In the events at 16,3, Allison reaches, takes, picks up and puts down, and she comments each time on what she is reaching for, taking, picking up or putting down. She either named the object (for example, "cookie" or "bag") or she commented on the fact that it was "more" or "gone", or she requested "more". In the events at 19,2 below, she does all of the same things as in the earlier sample (reaching, taking, picking up and putting down), but now it is striking that the words she uses comment on some aspect of the situation IN RELATION TO the object itself that she picks up, reaches for, offers, etc. She picked up or pointed to my CUP, but she said either "juice" or "Mommy", or "juice/ Mommy":

II: 63, 64, 65, 66 (19,2)

(A offering cookie to M)	Mommy/
Oh, thank you.	
(M taking cookie)	cookie/
Thank you.	
(A looking at empty cups)	juice/
Juice?	
Shall we have some juice? (M shaking juice can)	
(A pointing inside cup)	cup/
In the cup?	
(A picks up one cup; picking up second cup; holding it up to M)	Mommy/ juice/
Mommy juice?	
(A putting cup down)	no/
(A shaking own cup)	baby!/
Baby.	
(A picking up M's cup; looking inside cup)	Mommy/ juice/
(A pretends to drink; returning empty cup to M)	juice/ Mommy/
Juice? Is there juice in that cup?	
	no/
No.	

(A watching M pour juice)   Mommy/
(A drinks own juice and pointing to M's
cup)   juice/ Mommy/
    Uh huh.

                                             juice/
    Juice.
(A drinks juice)

Allison still named the object of her attention at 19,2, but when she did, it was in succession with another word that was related to it by virtue of some other aspect of the situation. Thus, she offered me a cookie, saying "Mommy", and then she said "cookie". She looked at the cups, saying "juice", and then pointed into the cup, saying "cup". Notice that it is not at all clear what aspect of Mommy or juice was relative to the cup. At one point, I asked her "Mommy juice?", and she said "no", putting down the cup she had held out to me, and shook her own cup, shouting "baby!". She then picked up my cup and looked inside it, saying "Mommy/ juice". She was evidently saying something about Mommy and juice relative to the cup, she clearly wanted the juice IN the cup, but whether she was talking about my pouring the juice or affirming my right to the juice in that particular cup could not be determined from the context or the utterance — even though 'instant replay' was available over and over again[31]. The interaction in the example below, from the third sample at 20,3, was considerably more complicated:

III: 45, 46 (20,3)
(A pointing to juice after drinking juice)   more juice/
(A picks up second cup)
    More juice?
(A offering one cup to M)   Mommy/
    What?

---

[31]   Refer to the transcript of the sample at 16,3 in the Appendix for event 27 and the use of "Mama" in relation to a second cup, after event 19 in the same sample. This appeared to be an early instance of what later became her dominant behavior at 19,2. But, again, note that it is not clear what she intended by her utterance "Mama" relative to the second cup.

(A looking at other cup in other hand)   Mommy/
  What? What?
(A giving cup to M)   Mommy juice/
  Mommy juice?
(M pouring juice into cup, A watching)   Allison!/ no!/
(A reaching out, trying to take cup from
M to pour juice back in container)   back/
  Oh, you want to pour it back.
(M keeping cup, starts to pour it back;
A gesturing 'pouring' with her left hand
into cup in her right hand)   mm/
(A transfers empty cup to her left hand;
and repeating the 'pouring' gesture, ends
up putting cup over her right hand)   baby/ juice/
  Baby juice?
(M puts down cup of juice, reaches for
A's cup)
  O.K. Allison needs some juice.
(M takes empty cup from A)
(A taking cup of juice from M)   Mommy/
(A noticing juice that M has spilled)   uh oh!/
  Uh oh.
(A smiles looking at juice spilled on floor) Mommy/
  What did Mommy do?
                                          spill/

Allison began with "more juice", pointing to the juice after she had
drunk juice, clearly wanting juice again. She also said "Mommy
juice" when giving a second cup to Mommy. However, what
followed ("Allison!/ no!/ back", her 'stopping' and 'pouring'
gestures with the cup in her hand, and "baby/ juice") seemed to
indicate that Allison wanted to do the pouring (instead of Mommy).
Note that I missed her intention at the time and Allison gave up;
first, she was attracted to the cup of juice ready to drink, and then
she noticed the spilled juice.

Allison was still talking about the juice, the cookies, and the cups in the second and third samples and she was still using only one word at a time. But, although she was still expressing certain of the same notions — having to do with objects, and actions with respect to objects — these same notions at 19,2 and 20,3 intersect with one another and with other notions as in "more", "no", "Baby" and "Mommy". She was using different kinds of words — more different substantive words occurred in the second and third examples than in the first. But more important, Allison was talking about the INTERRELATION among objects and events at 19,2 and 20,3, and not just commenting on a particular object or action in relation to itself as at 16,3.

There seems to be little question that the single words that have been described here are not different from the single-word utterances described so often in the literature. Indeed, it is precisely the kind of utterances that occurred at 19,2 that are described most often in the literature as holophrases or one-word sentences. Allison was talking about the relations between objects and events in her experience, but such relational notions were yet to be mapped onto longer utterances. Given her obvious awareness of such inter-actions among objects and events, if Allison knew anything about grammar, it seems that she would have said sentences. But she did not say sentences — even though she knew enough words, and she had earlier given evidence that she could produce two 'words' in ordered juxtaposition. One cannot then conclude that the utterances in the above examples depended upon or derived from underlying representations of basic GRAMMATICAL relationship, as suggested by McNeill or Smith, or representations of the SEMANTIC STRUCTURES of words as suggested by Ingram[32].

The twelve-month period from 9 to 21 months during which Allison used single-word utterances was marked by developmental change in both the form and function of words. Allison was on the verge of using syntax at 21 months only because she had, after considerable time, begun to achieve an awareness of the inter-

[32] David McNeill, *The acquisition of language*, 1970; Joshua Smith, "The development and structure of holophrases", 1970; David Ingram, "Transitivity in child language", 1971.

section of aspects of a situation in terms of certain recurring relations among objects,· events, and people (including herself). Such relations in the real world are ultimately coded by language; that is, one can analyze a linguistic code in order to describe and explain the linguistic representations of such relations. But there appears to be a false logic in the claim that single words that were related by virtue of behavior and situational context alone were dependent for their use upon an underlying linguistic representation. In sum, Allison did not use syntax, and it must be concluded that she was limited to one word at a time primarily because she did not know very much about sentences — about the structure of language.

In summary, the kinds of words that Allison used differed at different times in the period from first words at 9-10 months to productive syntax at 22 months. In roughly the first half of this period (until approximately 17 months), she used many different words, but not all words occurred consistently and repeatedly in her speech. It has been largely taken for granted, in the literature, that the words children acquire and use as single-word utterances are most often NOUN forms in the model language. And, indeed, there are more adult-noun words than any other 'part of speech' in the lexicon reported for the first video sample of Allison's speech at 16,3. However, when both relative frequency and relative persistence of different words in the first half of her second year were taken into account, it was fairly clear that, contrary to what one might have expected, Allison was not acquiring a vocabulary of substantive words. The words "more", "there", "gone", "away", "stop", "up", and "uh oh" were the dominant words in her speech before and at 16 months.

Learning the names for objects depends upon perceiving and discriminating among figurative aspects of 'things', so that certain things form a class. The mental representations of such a class of things would be a summary of perceptual attributes such that new members of the class could be recognized and included. Apparently, this was more difficult (in this period of time — roughly the first half of the second year) than organizing experiences of perceptually different objects according to salient and recurring behaviors which they have in common. This would follow, given what we know about the development of sensory-motor intelligence. Allison used words that referred to particular behaviors which occurred regularly, with many different objects which had little in common EXCEPT that they existed, disappeared, recurred, could be picked up, could be touched, *etc.* It appears that the summary mental representation of a class of objects that can be mapped onto a linguistic form or word is a later and somehow more difficult achievement, dependent, as has been already argued, on the achievement of object constancy in the end of the second year.

The use of function words to apply across classes of objects may be similar to the early instances of over-inclusion of word reference that have been described (as with the example "nénin" from Guillaume). It is possible that such early over-inclusion of reference, in the same period of time when relational, function words dominate in the use of speech, may represent a search for words that link experiences which are associated together by the child according to various criteria. That is, the child uses a word to link diverse experiences that may be more or less idiosyncratically related (according to figurative, functional, and affective criteria), as he searches for and attempts to discriminate regularities in his experience.

Sinclair[33] has recently related children's use of single-word utterances to the abstract action patterns or schemas formed by the child during the sensory-motor period described by Piaget. She described the early words in this period as representing the "organizing activity" of the child as opposed to the (presumably later) "denominational utterances" which have to do with the knowledge of objects. Both "organizing activity" and "object knowledge" form the essence of sensory-motor intelligence. Sinclair appears to be referring to precisely the same kinds of development as have been described here in terms of the use of functional and substantive words.

[33] Hermina Sinclair, "The transition from sensory-motor behavior to symbolic activity", *Interchange*, 1970.

The functional, relational, operational terms such as "there", "more", "away", "gone", "up", "uh oh" reflect the organizing activity of the child, and characterize sensory-motor intelligence and language development up to the second half of the second year. The early over-inclusion of words like Guillaume's "nénin" (as discussed in Chapter 4) may represent the same kind of organizing activity. On the other hand, the accepted, conventional use of substantive or denominational terms depends upon knowledge of objects. Not surprisingly, such words are a later development with the achievement of object constancy. It has been argued here that learning such words depends upon the child's ability to conceptually represent the objects to which the words make reference. That is, one cannot 'know a word' such as "dog" in terms of semantic representation until one has an idea of what dogs ARE and of their existence in time and space, independently of oneself and one's actions.

To conclude, it is inappropriate to think of children learning adult 'parts of speech' in the course of their development before the use of syntax. Rather it is the case that children develop certain conceptual representations of regularly recurring experiences, and then learn whatever words conveniently code or linguistically represent such conceptual notions. Thus, it is only coincidental that, in the adult model, "see" and "stop" are 'verbs'; "there", "more", and "away" are 'adverbs'; and "up" is a 'preposition'. Children learn to talk about their experience of the world; descriptions of the words that they use in terms of adult 'parts of speech' are superficial and misleading.

In the final chapter, the words that children use when they say only one word at a time will be related to the subsequent emergence of grammar, and consideration will be given to the possible potential for the induction of different notions of syntax at different times in the development from first words to phrases.

CONCEPTS, WORDS, AND SENTENCES

5.1. CONCEPTUAL NOTIONS UNDERLYING SINGLE-WORD UTTERANCES AND THE ORIGIN OF GRAMMAR

What is it that children DO know in this period of time when, it is claimed, they do not know the language code? Returning to the discussion of the conceptual relations underlying early two- and three-word sentences, there are several conclusions that can be drawn about the origin of such conceptual notions in the use of single-word utterances. It is clear, to begin with, that the conceptual notions encoded in early sentences do not originate with the use of structured speech. Further, a theory to explain the transition to syntactic speech would depend upon an explanation of children's learning several aspects of a theory of grammar (for example, as manifested by the distinction in children's early sentences between FUNCTIONAL and GRAMMATICAL relations described in Chapter 2), and the aspects of grammar that are learned first are no doubt largely determined by the conceptual notions underlying single-word utterances. However, not only does the learning of early aspects of grammar derive from the conceptual notions underlying single-word utterances, but such conceptions are apparently of different kinds, which may help to explain certain apparent differences in strategies for learning grammar among different children.

5.1.1. *The Use of Function Forms and the 'Pivotal Aspect' of Early Syntax*

It was reported that certain function forms, for example, "more", "no", "there", "away", and "up" predominated in Allison's speech at 10 to 17 months and have been reported as occurring persistently and often in the pre-syntax speech of children studied by early diarists, for example, Guillaume and Leopold. Each was a constant form, that is, the same word was used in different situations that shared features of context and behavior, for example, "more" in reference to another instance of an object; "away" in reference to an object that had or was about to disappear, *etc.* Each appeared to specify an identifiable cognitive notion — such as existence, disappearance, recurrence, 'upness'. Such words represented certain recurring aspects of behavior and of objects in the child's experience.

Linguistically, the potential juxtaposition of such forms as these with other forms could generally be predicted from the context in which they occurred. When Allison said "more" as she reached for another cookie, it was not difficult to predict the connection between the words "more" and "cookie"; and, indeed, utterances like "more cookie" occurred from time to time. When such two-word utterances as "more cookie" occurred — in Allison's pre-syntax speech as well as in the early syntactic speech of Kathryn, Eric and Gia — the nature of the relation between the two words derived from the relational nature of the word with constant form and consistent use in each repeated situation (of existence, non-existence, recurrence, *etc.*). That is, the meaning of the relationship between the words was dependent upon the meaning of one of the words — for example, "more", "no", "up", or "a'gone". It was concluded that Allison's early sporadic two-word utterances were not manifestations of an underlying rule system but, rather, were a manifestation of the essentially transitive nature of the notions coded by the particular forms "more", "away", "stop", *etc.*, to the nonlinguistic states of affairs to which they referred. SOMETHING had to STOP; there had to be SOMETHING to RECUR; SOMETHING DISAPPEARED, *etc.*

At age 16 months, when Allison produced two-word utterances with "wídə", "more", and "away" she might have acquired a strategy for juxtaposing such words as these with other words as she learned them, with the resulting 'pivotal' characteristic of structured speech described by Braine[1]. It seems fairly clear that this is precisely what Eric and the three boys described by Braine did do. Braine described early syntactic speech as pivotal in reference to the form and distribution of linguistic elements. Some words (pivots) occurred more often, in fixed position, and with a larger number of different words than did other words (x-words). It has been pointed out that the pivot grammar account of child speech is, essentially, a superficial description of the relative distribution of different words that the child uses[2].

There appear to be important differences among children in the extent to which the distributional phenomenon actually exists in their early syntax. The distribution itself — the fact that some words occur more often in combination with other words — derives from the two facts that (1) certain forms make reference to what appear to be predominant distinctions in the child's experience, and so come to be used more often and in more varied situations, and (2) such distinctions are inherently relational or transitive in nature, having to do with many and different objects and events. Such differences among children in the extent of pivotal distribution in their early sentences, and the relevance of so-called pivotal structures for representation of certain notions children have about objects and events in the world may explain different strategies for the transition from single words to syntax. It appears that the use of such relational function forms and their eventual syntactic combination may dominate as a strategy for emerging grammar among certain children at certain times.

Children may learn such function forms first, and learn to use them as single-word utterances, each in different situations that have critical features of context and behavior in common. As they learn to speak and understand other words relevant to those same or similar situations, the cooccurrence of both functional and substantive features of events can be represented — that is, both

[1]   Martin D. S. Braine, "The ontogeny of English phrase structure", 1963.
[2]   See Lois Bloom, "Why not pivot grammar?", 1971; Lois Bloom, *Language development*, 1970, 222-227; Melissa Bowerman, "Learning to talk", 1970; and Roger Brown, "*A first language*", in prep.

"more" and "cookie" in the instance of another cookie. Thus, such functional conceptual notions as existence, nonexistence, recurrence, 'upness', etc., that underlie the use of certain single-word utterances, appear to predominate in the child's organization of experience at a particular stage. As a result, certain children, at this point, may go on to productively combine such words as these with other words. Their early syntax, then, would appear to depend on the linguistic induction that such function words combine with others words in a direct and linear relation, and the meaning relation between the two words derives from the meaning of the function word. There is a linear, one-to-one correspondence between the meanings of such words and the relational meanings between such words combined with other words. For example, the meaning of "more" and the meaning of "cookie" (in a situation of 'another cookie' or 'cookie again') are the same meanings of each word in the utterance "more cookie". The changes in the transitions from these words as single words, to these words appearing successively, to the syntactic utterance "more cookie" have to do with explicitness of reference. There is no new relation expressed precisely because — and only because — of the inherently relational meaning of words like "more". Further, such syntactic relations can be considered 'context-bound', in the sense that there cannot be existence, disappearance, recurrence, 'upness', etc., unless there is SOMETHING that exists, disappears, recurs, is up, etc. "There" cannot make reference unless something is there; "away" is meaningless unless something disappears, etc.

This first linguistic induction can be summarized as follows:

(i)   Certain conceptions of experience are coded by words which have meaning only in relation to other words that refer to objects or actions on objects. The combination of such words with other words is direct, linear, and context-bound, and not determined by relationship between intervening linguistic categories. The meaning of the relationship in such two-word sentences is dependent upon the meaning of one of the words in combination.

All of the conceptions underlying such words as these do not come together to constitute a cognitive category as such; rather, each is a distinctive cognitive notion. Thus, there is no basis in terms of content, experience, or meaning to justify the assertion that such word-forms are subsumed within a linguistic category that would specify structural relationship. Such words do form a class by virtue of distributional criteria alone, only AFTER they are combined with other words in speech. The meaning of the words entails relationship, and their occurrence in two-word utterances makes the relation explicit. For reasons that are not at all clear, Allison (and, apparently, Kathryn and Gia as well) did not make the above induction. The productivity of such phrases was expected to occur in Allison's speech — after their earlier sporadic occurrence — but failed to materialize. When Allison, Kathryn and Gia did indeed present evidence of linguistic inductions about grammar, each at about age 21 to 22 months, they were apparently inductions of a different sort.

5.1.2. *Conceptual Relationships and Early Linguistic Categories*

The words that began to predominate in Allison's use of single-word utterances at 17 months have been described in terms of their substantive, figurative aspects. It was proposed that Allison was able to use such words, at this time, to make reference to objects because she had reached the point in sensory-motor development at which such cognitive functions as perception and imagery could result in the mental summary representations of enduring objects. However, it was not possible to describe the conceptual functions of such words in relation to the total events in which they occurred with the same confidence as the words like "more", "away", and "stop", which were relatively unambiguous in the situations in which they occurred. There was no way of knowing if Allison perceived the same relationships among persons, objects, and events as might an adult in the same situations, or that her single words (whether or not successive) occurred with the same semantic 'structure' as might the same words, spoken by an adult, in the same situation.

The intersecting aspects of experience that the children talked about with successive single-word utterances included certain recurring RELATIONSHIPS among persons, objects, and events. That is, although the objects and events in experience — and the words that made reference in the same situations — were different and varied, the relationships among the objects and events were few in number and recurred often. It is proposed that such relations themselves become represented as COGNITIVE categories which form the basis for the child's semantic learning, as words are mapped onto such mental representations. As words occur in relation to categories of mental schemas and in relation to one another, the child learns the possible meaning relations that can occur among them. Learning syntax, then, would be a matter of learning to code the relationships in experience in terms of the structural relationships between categories of WORDS in utterances. Thus, it was not simply that the children needed to perceive the relative position of words in adult utterances as proposed by Braine, and Smith and Braine[3]. Rather, combinations of different words represented hierarchical structures in which meaning derived from the relationship between the words, and not from the meanings of the individual words or their relative position in adult utterances.

Such words as person and object names occurred in situations in which events happened, objects were acted upon, and persons did things or were otherwise associated with objects. Certain recurring events were the same, regardless of the different persons or objects that participated in the events. For example, "Mama", "Dada", "Mimi", and "Baby" could all be agents in their relation to such different objects as "meat", "shoe", "suitcase", *etc.*, in the situations in which they occurred. In the two-word and three-word sentences with substantive forms (described earlier for older children), the nature of the grammatical relationship between subject and predicate, or among agent, action, and goal or object was not apparent from the words themselves. Different words occurred

---

[3] Martin D. S. Braine, "On learning the grammatical order of words", *Psychological Review*, 1963, and Kirk Smith and Martin D. S. Braine, "Artificial language learning and language acquisition", in press.

with the same function; there was not an invariable form for representing a grammatical function such as 'subject' or 'object'. The meaning of grammatical relationship (such as Agent-Action, Possessive, Locative) was independent of the lexical meanings of either of the words, and different words could be combined with the same grammatical meaning. That is, both "Mommy" and "sock", "Daddy" and "briefcase", and "Baby" and "shoe" can have the same meaning relation between them (e.g. the possessive). In order to use a linguistic code to talk about (or to understand others talking about) the perceived relations among persons and objects in changing states of affairs, it is necessary to know that different words can mean the same thing in relation to other words with which they occur. Such words form LINGUISTIC categories, then, based on their meaning in relation to other words.

The linguistic notions of grammatical relationship represent relationships between categories that are defined in terms of formal linguistic criteria. Such linguistic criteria specify certain conditions of arrangement and cooccurrence, for example, which define the structural relationship of categories to each other. There is no evidence before the use of syntax that single-word utterances represent GRAMMATICAL categories. But there is evidence — particularly, the use of successive single-word utterances within a single speech event — to conclude that single-word utterances do represent certain COGNITIVE categories that are derived from the child's experience of relationship among persons, objects, and events.

The cognitive categories that result from development in the first two years, and that form the basis for discovering grammatical categories, are networks of relations which the child has come to represent in thought. The 'holistic' structure of events with successive single-word utterances provided some evidence of the categorical representation of whole events. There are, no doubt, different cognitive categories for the representation of different kinds of relations in experience. Some events are more similar to each other than they are to other events. For example, certain events can be marked as 'locating' events, others as 'persons moving' events, others as 'persons affecting objects' events, etc. Moreover, there is overlap among cognitive categories of experience because the same or similar people and objects participate in the same and different kinds of events. Part of the difficulty in learning the linguistic code is probably due to such representation of the same and similar objects and persons in different categories of events, because of their participation in different networks of relationship.

The child perceives and comes to represent different kinds of events as he is learning the words he needs for understanding and talking about them. Adults talk to the child about such events, and the child hears words in combination that refer to the categories of events that he has come to represent conceptually. The child comes to discover the semantic relations that can exist between words by hearing such words in relation to each other, in relation to the events in which they occur, and using such words successively in the same kinds of situations. Different words can refer to the same aspect of a particular relation, when the same relation occurs in different situations, for example, Mommy ('s) sock, Daddy ('s) briefcase, *etc.* But, further, the same words can also be used in different relations in other situations.

Once the child begins to understand and use words relative to the total cognitive relation or category, words can begin to assume SEMANTIC significance in relation to one another. Having learned the meanings of words as representing enduring objects, he learns the meaning relations between words when a whole event (eventually a cognitive category) is mapped onto several, as yet linguistically unrelated, words. Using and understanding words in this way gives the child the beginning clues for learning about the possible meaning relations that can exist between words. When different words coincide in their meaning relations with other words, that is, when different words such as "Mommy", "Daddy", "Baby", *etc.* mean the same thing IN RELATION TO other words, the child has the basis for formulating a linguistic category of these words relative to other categories of words.

Linguistic categories, then, contain words that form classes by virtue of their shared meaning relation to other words. Learning syntax depends upon the child's learning the ORDER of linguistic categories relative to one another, and children learn to sequence categories of words, NOT individual words. The categories AGENT-OF-ACTION or PERSON-AFFECTED, for example, are linguistic categories that are formed because different words come together in their meaning relation with other words, which similarly form other linguistic classes. They are semantic categories that depend upon and derive from the meaning relations between words. They are not cognitive categories. The child does not have a cognitive notion AGENT or PERSON-AFFECTED; rather, his cognitive categories are mental representations of the entire relation in experience between agent-action-object or person affected-affecting state, *etc.*

This view contrasts with the theory proposed by Schlesinger in a fundamental way. Schlesinger recognized that certain cognitive notions or relationships are the input to grammar learning. He proposed that such notions as agent and object were the cognitive notions which are somehow 'realized' in early sentences.[4] However, the notion of AGENT is a linguistic category and it represents a category of words that relates to other categories of words. Cognitive categories do not develop in a one-to-one correspondence with eventual linguistic categories; that is, the cognitive categories that are formed in the last half of the second year are not directly mapped onto corresponding linguistic categories. It is proposed here that the cognitive category is the whole relationship that exists independently of the words that are used in understanding and representing the relationship in speech.

In sum, it is proposed that a second induction for learning grammar depends on something like the following chronology of events: (1) Perceiving and participating in certain action schemas, with single-word utterances occurring as successive chainings, as each word comments on or refers to the object or movement that holds the child's attention. (2) The ability to hold a whole event in mind. with successive single-word utterances beginning to occur in holistic networks that include different aspects of relations in such events. (3) Awareness of meaning relations between words as the child begins to understand and use words in relation to such

[4]   I. M. Schlesinger, "Production of utterances and language acquisition", 1971.

holistic representation of events, and begins to develop semantic categories of words. (4) Awareness of the relative ORDER between such semantic categories for coding the meaning relations that linguistically represent the cognitive categories of events in thought[5]. The strategy for learning grammar that Allison, Kathryn, and Gia presumably used involved the following alternative induction:

(ii)   Certain conceptions of experience form cognitive categories of events that are coded by the interrelation among different linguistic categories of substantive words, forming structural relationships with distinctive meanings. Such structural meanings are independent of the lexical meanings of the forms within categories.

Coding the relationship of such conceptions as, for example, agent, action, and goal of action, involves formulating the linguistic categories for representing words relative to one another. There is a necessary intervening step (the formation of linguistic categories), between the prior cognitive distinctions (that ultimately underlie linguistic categories), and the eventual sequencing of lexical items in the surface structure of utterances.

In summary, children learn different conceptual notions, for example, as indicated by "more" or "Mommy", and it can be hypothesized that the mental representations of experience of these notions differ. For example, Mommy is the agent, the doer, the actor of events — and exists in a situation as an instance of X in the relationship $[x' \ (y')]$ — where it is the particular interrelation between x' AND y' that specifies x' as agent. In contrast, "more" represents the notion A which is manifested in α instances of X, Y, and Z — that is, the relationship $\alpha[x']$ — where it is the meaning of α and the particular relation of α TO x' that specifies the underlying conceptual notion. Thus, there are different kinds of experience, and it appears to follow that their mental representations

---

[5]   This proposed chronology and the implication of 'awareness' on the child's part is meant, certainly, as description of implicit, rather than explicit, knowledge.

differ. It should not be surprising, therefore, that such representations are coded differently by the language as well.

It is just such differences in coding mental conceptions of experience that are manifested by the different aspects of a theory of grammar that are apparently learned towards the end of the second year[6]. However, as has already been pointed out, the alternative strategies that have been proposed were not actually mutually exclusive — both seemed to be manifest in varying extent in the speech of different children. Eric and the children described by Braine[7] appeared to use a strategy for learning grammar that involved using certain constant forms, with recurrent function, in direct, linear juxtaposition with other words. The mapping of such underlying conceptual notions onto syntactic utterances was fairly direct — the surface structure was the only structure. Induction (i) predominated in this early syntax learning. Allison appeared to have the potential for such a strategy at one time, as evidenced by utterances with "wídə", "more", and "away" at 16 months. However, the combination of several factors, including, perhaps, increased awareness of phenomenological relationships in experience and the availability of a larger number of words, operated somehow to alter that strategy if not cause her to abandon it entirely. Induction (ii) predominated in the early syntax learning of Allison, Kathryn, and Gia.

5.1.3. *Allison's Emerging Grammar at Time IV, Age 22 months*

The emergence of grammar has already been described for Gia and Kathryn.[8] While the 40 minute sample of Allison's speech at

---

[6] In Heinz Werner and Bernard Kaplan, *Symbol formation*, 1963, there is similar analysis of two different kinds of early word combinations that are developmentally ordered. They reported that, in early combinations, two elements in an utterance "refer to the same presented event" and the total expression is not far removed from a single-word expression. "On the other hand, the two elements of the second two-unit utterance emphasize different features of the presented event" (147 and ff.).

[7] Martin D. S. Braine, "The ontogeny of English phrase structure", 1963.

[8] In Lois Bloom, *Language development*, 1970.

22 months cannot provide enough evidence for proposing a grammar, it is abundantly clear that Allison had learned something about syntax.

There was a marked decrease in the total number of utterances in the fourth sample. There were 335 utterances at 16.3; 321 utterances at 19,2; 379 utterances at 20,3; and 271 utterances at 22 months. However, at Time IV almost half of the utterances consisted of 2 or more words; her longest utterance contained 6 words. Allison had used more utterances at 19 and 20 months to talk about some of the same kinds of things that she was able to combine 2 and 3 utterances to talk about at 22 months. Words that referred separately to objects and events and were contextually related earlier, were now linguistically related as well.

The mean length of utterances in the sample was 1.73 morphemes, and it appeared that Allison had passed beyond the two-word utterance limit that prevails in child speech when mean length of utterance is less than 1.5. Two-word utterances occurred, of course, and expressed agent-action, action-object, possessive, locative, and attributive relations between words (attributives, for example, (10) "chocolate chip cookie", and (72) "pony dress"; and locative particles with verbs, for example (54) "step in", and (60) "walking around" were restricted in that each tended to occur only with particular nouns or verbs). However, although verb-object occurred 33 times and subject-verb occurred 18 times, all three basic grammatical relations were expressed in 13 subject-verb-object strings. Thus, an important difference between Allison's speech with mean length of utterance 1.73 and the early sentences from Gia and Kathryn when mean length of utterance was 1.3 is that the full underlying representation of subject-verb-object was beginning to be manifest in her speech.

There was a total of 31 different verb forms that occurred in multiword utterances (counting forms with and without "-ing" as a single form). The verbs that occurred with noun forms were always single and unmodified; that is, there were no concatenatives, auxiliaries (except for -ing), or negation. Almost $2/3$ of the different verbs occurred only with direct object nouns; almost $1/3$ occurred both with and without an object noun; and only 3 verbs never occurred with an object noun. Three verbs took only animate nouns as objects: "help", "peeking", and "pull"; all of the other object-taking verbs occurred with only inanimate nouns as objects. Except for two ambiguous sentences with "wait", there were no verbs that occurred with both animate and inanimate nouns as objects. In contrast, approximately 90% of the nouns that functioned as sentence-subject were animate. Thus, there was a distinction between animate and inanimate nouns in their distribution before and after verb forms. None of the subject nouns was modified; that is, sentence-subjects consisted only of single nouns, for example "Mommy", "Baby" (to refer to herself, or her doll), "Baby Allison", "horse", etc. There were no pronouns.

Whereas sentence-subjects occurred less often and consisted of an unmodified noun that was most often animate, the structure of the predicate was more varied. There were two possible ways in which predicate structures were more complex than simple verb-object, and these were, in effect, mutually exclusive. The embedding of the possessive phrase after the verb occurred, and the inclusion of both object noun and adverbs after the verb occurred, but both complexities did not occur within the bounds of a single sentence. There were six utterances in which a person name appeared in relation to an object noun after a verb. In three of these, Allison was the actor: (20) "wiping baby chin", (15) "eat Mommy cookie", and "eating Mommy cookie", and the relation after the verb was possessive; Allison was indeed wiping her own chin, and eating Mommy's cookie. In two others, Allison was again the actor: (11) "get Mommy cookie", and (23) "pour Mommy juice", but neither the cookie nor the juice was present as yet. The function of "Mommy" in (11) and (23) was equivocal; although the possessive was most likely, an indirect object interpretation was possible. (75) "there baby cup" also occurred as Allison took a cup from Mommy for juice for herself. These six utterances were evidence of an important grammatical development — two words in one structural relation that was embedded within a higher level structure.

The second added complexity in the predicate was the use of

adverbials that included locative phrases, with predicates that included both verbs and objects. For example, (65) "drink apple juice right here", (75) "drink apple juice again", (51) "help cow in table". In (32) "put away Allison bag", the object was not expressed, but the locative was a possessive phrase, "Allison bag".

Thus, three aspects of syntax distinguished Allison's speech in this sample, when mean length of utterance was 1.73 morphemes, from linguistically earlier child speech limited to two-word utterances, with mean length of utterance less than 1.5 morphemes: subject-verb-object strings, and expansion of the predicate by either embedding one structural relation, such as the possessive, within the predicate, or the inclusion of both object noun and a locative or "again" after a verb. However, when the object of a verb was a phrase, or when both object and locative phrase occurred, there was no sentence-subject expressed. Further, both kinds of expansion, that is, both a possessive object phrase and a locative, did not occur within a single predicate with a verb.

There were, then, specific constraints on the surface form of utterances. More than half of the utterances were single words, but although three and four word sentences occurred, the number of sentence positions that could be filled was limited to three, and there was a necessary reduction in surface structure with expansion of the predicate. Sentence-subjects were most vulnerable to reduction when something had to be eliminated as, for example, in the following sequence:

IV: 51 (22)

(A had tried to pull a truck with a cow on
it from under the table where M had
pushed it; turning towards M for help)   Mommy//
                                            Mommy pull/
                                            help cow/ cow/

Mommy what?   pull cow in___/
Mommy___(M interrupting A)   pull cow/
What should Mommy do?   help cow in table/
Pull cow in table?   mhmm/

With successive utterances, Allison both expanded and reduced what she said. The first two utterances in the sequence, "Mommy" and "Mommy pull", made it quite clear that "Mommy" was expected to act in a particular way on the cow that was under the table, but Allison could not quite get it all together.

Successive single-word utterances were explained at 19,2 and 20,3 by the fact that Allison did not know the code for specifying the semantic-syntactic relationships between words. She apparently did not know those structures which might have linguistically represented the relationships among objects and events that seemed to be conceptually related in mental representation. And, indeed, although it was not possible to identify a one to one correspondence between relations among successive single-word utterances at 19,2 and 20,3 and the relations in the syntactic structures at 22 months, it is evident that many of the same kinds of conceptual relations were represented in both the earlier successive single-word utterances and the subsequent sentences. If Allison was limited to one word at a time because she did not know the code at Times II and III, then what could explain the occurrence of successive utterances at Time IV?

Thirty speech events contained successive utterances (both single and multi-word utterances) that were not chained by successive actions or utterances addressed to Allison. Of these 30, 10 were sequences in which the relations among the separate utterances were the same as those relations expressed syntactically elsewhere in the corpus; these occurred in events (5), (7), (8), (19), (24), (30), (41), (45), (71), and (76). Of these, (5), (7), and (8), contain the words "baby", "eat", and "cookies", which were combined elsewhere as "baby eat", "eat cookies", and "baby eat cookies". In (19), "baby" and "cookie" each occurred several times as Allison was eating crumbs.

In the remaining 20 events, there appeared to be two constraints that prevented Allison from conjoining successive utterances within a single utterance. Either Allison did not know the relevant grammatical structure, for example, in (20) for specifying the instrument of an action (her dress which she called "lap") or, she was unable to express all possible relations within a single utterance, for example, in (43) including "again" in a subject-verb-object string.

Certain other sequences that occurred were considerably more complex and would have required correspondingly complex linguistic structure to render them comprehensible without the strong support of context and behavior. For example, in (38) it is not clear who "baby" is; if Allison was referring to herself as "baby" and the doll as "baby doll", then what she wanted was for Mommy to help baby (Allison) with the baby doll. In (60), Allison was specifying the means necessary, "standing up" and "walking around", for gaining an end, "cookie", as she stood up and then walked around to get the cookie that she evidently had in mind from the outset.

Finally, the clearest examples of utterances occurring successively because of syntactic constraints are in the two events (58) and (59), where Allison first recounted and then reenacted an immediately preceding incident:

IV: 58, 59 (22)
(A puts pig in truck as she squats over
  truck)
(A starts to sit on truck; sharp corner hits
  her bottom; A pushes truck away)
(A touching sharp corner of truck with
  her finger)   bang/
(A pointing to her back)   baby back/
  Bang baby back?
(A pointing to sharp corner)   sharp/
  Oh, it's sharp? Oh, I see. Yes it is sharp.

                                                 baby ride truck!/

  Baby ride truck? Can you ride that
  truck?

                                                 sharp/

  It's sharp. So you have to be careful.
(A putting hand on back)   back/
  What's on your back?

(A putting pig to sharp corner of truck)	pig/ pig/
(A pulling pig back to her)	sharp!/
Oh, it's sharp.	
(A showing pig to M; 'twisting' at its tail)	pig/ pig/ pig/ pig/
What — What's that? What is that?	
That's the pig's —	
(A pointing to pig's tail)	hurt knee/
Oh, he hurt his knee?	
(A pointing to truck)	hurt/ hurt truck/
Hurt truck? Did he hurt his knee?	
Or did he hurt the —	
	be careful!/
Be —	
(A pointing to truck)	sharp!/
Be careful! It's sharp! Yes, please be careful.	

When Allison reenacted the incident using the pig — symbolic behavior that has been described so often by Piaget — it was clear that she knew what had happened to her. But, she could not bring together all of these relations among person affected, instrument, attribute, location, cause, effect, etc., within a single sentence or several sentences because she simply did not, as yet, know enough about grammar. Most of the successive utterances at 22 months referred to event relationships that Allison did not yet know how to code linguistically.

There is substantial evidence of both semantic and syntactic structure in early child sentences. Semantically, the relations between words include only a limited set of the meaning relations that are possible in the language. Utterances are not merely echoes of adult speech or shadows of events in context. The words that come together in such meaning relations form semantic categories that are remarkably well-defined in terms of function, but such categories are still few in number and include only a limited number of possible words as members. Syntactically, there is also only a limited set of structures represented in speech. But the more important evidence that children have learned grammar is the fact that the structure of their sentences is influenced by several constraints that are highly systematic.

5.1.4. *From Single Words to Syntax*

To return to the original questions, what is it that children do know in the period of time before using syntax, and what explains the transition from single-word utterances to two- and three-word structured utterances? Learning syntax is not adequately explained by the theory that children learn the relative order of particular words — the same words occur everywhere in the stream of speech they hear. Moreover, and significantly, Allison presented evidence of knowing something about the relative word order of certain words at 16 months (utterances with "wídə"), but she did not use word order to code meaning relationships between words until five months later at 21-22 months of age. Nor does the evidence from artificial language learning support the theory of 'pivot grammar' as the natural outcome of position learning and the first step in language development[9]. Artificial languages are devised according to rules of relative position — there are no other criteria for combination of units (such as possible meaning relationships between them). It should not be surprising, then, that relative position is precisely what is retrieved from exposure to permitted artificial language utterances. But the distributional phenomena in early child utterances are apparently motivated by conceptual considerations. Words occur together in natural language structure because of the nature of the meaning relationships between them, and artificial languages make no provision for relationship between items.

Further, the view that language development results from prior linguistic knowledge of the nature of sentences as proposed by McNeill, cannot be taken as hypothesis or theory until such prior linguistic knowledge is identified or otherwise described. There is

---

[9] As argued in Kirk Smith and Martin D. S. Braine, "Artificial language learning and language acquisition", in press.

an important distinction between the innate propensity or capacity to acquire language and the idea that such innate capacity takes the form of linguistic notions of either form or substance. There is simply no evidence that children have knowledge of linguistic structure before they use structure in their speech. The period in Allison's development from first words to the productive use of syntax was a period of change in both the kinds of words she used and the way in which she used them. If one believes, with Piaget, that developmental change occurs as a function of the child's manipulating and interacting with his environment, then the idea that single-word utterances reflect prior linguistic knowledge of sentences becomes even less tenable.

Children need to observe underlying regularities in experience and represent these somehow in terms of conceptual relations between persons, objects and events. Thus, the child first learns that persons like Mommy act and that objects like doors or carrots are acted upon — and not merely that "Mommy" occurs and then "door" occurs. Children no doubt make certain cognitive distinctions first and proceed to analyze the speech they hear in relevant nonlinguistic contexts on the basis of such prior distinctions. Learning relative position of words with specific grammatical function is a critical aspect of a child's first theory of a grammar, but grammatical function depends upon underlying cognitive function. There have been reports of alternative orders in the speech of different children — where order may not match order in the model or be otherwise predictable[10]. Early alternative orders of mention in speech may represent an hypothesis-testing in which the child may express concepts on the basis of temporal order, saliency, or focus, in much the same way as in occurrence of successive single-word utterances. As pointed out earlier, such utterances provide evidence that the child can hold two things together in a single proposition — a psychological requirement for first sentences — although he still has not learned the code.

[10] See, for example, Martin D. S. Braine, "The acquisition of language in infant and child", 1970, and Oscar Bloch's description of alternative word order in the speech of his three children, in "La phrase dans le langage de l'enfant", 1924.

Thus, the use of syntactic speech depends upon several things, first of which is an awareness of certain basic phenomena: things exist, cease to exist, and recur; objects are acted upon or otherwise located or owned; persons do things. This kind of awareness probably represents part of what children do know in this period when they use only one word at a time, and such knowledge is not linguistic in origin or in substance. The eventual use of syntax next depends on knowledge of word forms that refer to aspects of experience, and children use and understand increasing numbers of different words in this period of time. And, ultimately, children need to distinguish between two alternative syntactic representations: (1) certain words have constant form and constant function and combine as immediate and linear constituents with other forms, and (2) certain other words, which differ in form, have common function in relation to other words, and their common function is the basis on which the child formulates linguistic categories which are hierarchical relative to each other.

Finally, it must be said that one cannot know the mind of a child with anything even approaching certainty or conviction. The study of the origin of the meanings of words and notions of grammar involves conjecture and inference about the nature of the child's mental representations and experience — which lead to tenuous conclusions at best. But children do speak and interact with their environment in certain ways that are consistent and therefore potentially predictable. The ways in which children use speech, the behaviors that accompany speech acts, and the features of context that precede, endure, or follow the act of speaking can be observed — and certain regularities between the form of utterances and their function can be identified thereby. Conclusions about the meanings of words and the origins of grammar, in this view, depend upon constancies in the USE of certain words. It is suggested that there is an important connection between the use of a word, in the sense proposed here, and its meaning for the child.

5.2. 'RICH' INTERPRETATION OF SYNTACTIC AND SINGLE-WORD CHILD UTTERANCES

The fact that young children talk about what they see and do has been exploited by several investigators who have taken what children mean by what they say seriously. In the earlier study of emerging grammar, information from context and behavior was used to infer the semantic intention of the children's utterances in order to explain their structure. Roger Brown has since dubbed this tactic a "rich interpretation" of utterances; quite simply, one infers more about the child's utterance than is possible when one considers only what the child actually says. When Kathryn sat on her mother's lap holding a rubber band, pushing at her hair and saying "Mommy pigtail", she intended her utterance to mean something about Mommy in relation to Kathryn's hair. Even though an actual verb did not occur, the underlying structure of such utterances as this included an intervening predicate relationship between the words that were actually said. 'Rich' interpretation provided PART of the evidence that was used for making this analysis. In the study of single-word utterances before syntax, structural meanings could not be attributed to the substantive words that occurred in the same way. This does not amount to a reversal of tactic or orientation, and it is important to elaborate on why it does not. The analysis presented here does not offer a different view of child language data; rather it is the data that are different.

Since the tactic of 'rich' interpretation was, in a sense, 'legitimized'[11], a number of other investigators have used it in studying the semantic development of children using single-word utterances — in the period before the use of syntax.[12] Their reasoning has gone something like this: if "Mommy pigtail" really means "Mommy

---

[11] After Lois Bloom, *Language development*, 1970; Roger Brown, "*A first language*", in prep.
[12] For example, Joshua Smith, "The development and structure of holophrases", 1970; David McNeill, *The acquisition of language*, 1970; Patricia Greenfield, Joshua Smith, Bernice Laufer, "Communication and the beginnings of language: the development of semantic structure in one-word speech and beyond", draft, 1972.

verb (*me*) pigtail", then just "Mommy" or just "pigtail" in the same
context, when the child is limited to only one word at a time, must
have the same underlying structure. Further, that a child will say
the same word in two different situations, for example, the single
word "light" when he sees the light and "light" when he wants to
turn on the light, provides evidence, in this view, that he knows
two different structures or 'meanings' corresponding to the two
different uses of the word. This last argument follows from the
interpretations of the homonymous pair "Mommy sock" in the
1970 syntax study, where Kathryn said "Mommy sock" when she
picked up Mommy's sock, and again when Mommy was putting
Kathryn's sock on Kathryn. But the analysis of "Mommy sock"
that resulted in two different structural descriptions (for Possessive
and Subject-Object) depended upon evidence that was far more
forceful than rich interpretation alone. Such evidence is available
when children use two and three word utterances and does not exist
with single-word utterances — no matter how rich the interpretation.

Evidence from 'rich' interpretation was only PART of the evidence that was used to analyze the structure of syntactic utterances in
the earlier study. There were, in addition, three other aspects of the
data which were no less important. First was the critical fact that
judgments of the children's knowledge of structural relationship
between words depended also upon what they SAID in the total
corpus of utterances — the actual linguistic data were significant
after all. In the example above, "Mommy pigtail", the underlying
predicate relation between the words depended upon an intervening
abstract constituent — in effect, a deleted verb. This analysis was
not offered on the basis of semantic interpretation alone, however.
It depended no less upon the fact that Kathryn had also presented
evidence that she knew about verbs — that verbs occurred in
relation to both nominal subject forms and direct object noun
forms. She said such things as "Mommy kiss" and "Mommy pull"
as well as "pull hat" and "eat meat"[13]. The occurrence of such

---

[13]   Lois Bloom, *Language development*, 1970, 46-47, and Chapter 6.

structural pairs did not depend on whether the verbs she knew were transitive or intransitive. Both kinds of verbs occurred, and transitive verbs occurred with subject or object nouns, but not with both in the same utterance.

In contrast, Eric rarely used nominal subject forms in relation to verbs and never in relation to other noun forms in the same period of time when the mean length of his utterances was less than 1.5. Thus a sentence-subject constituent could not be provided for in an account of what Eric knew about grammar — even though it was possible to include an agent in the semantic interpretation of several of his utterances. Similarly, in the first corpus of speech collected from Gia, she produced no verb forms. Even though one could observe an action when Gia produced certain noun plus noun utterances, these could not be structurally described as subject–object strings (as they were in the second corpus six weeks later, when verbs did indeed occur in her speech in relation to subject and object nouns). The point is that the linguistic data — the entire corpus of speech — revealed important complementing regularities which were certainly as necessary as the semantic interpretations inferred for individual utterances. In order to be able to say that the children knew something about structural relationship (such as subject-object or subject-verb) or semantic relationship (such as agent-object or agent-action), the linguistic data would have to include such utterances as "Mommy pull" and "Mommy hat" as well as "pull hat".

The second feature of the syntactic data from Kathryn, Eric and Gia was the fact that the ORDER in which the words occurred corresponded to the word order which, in the adult model, signals such relationships as possession and agent-object of an action. It was possible, then, to attribute grammatical function to the words in a two- or three-word utterance because words were ordered in sentences and the ORDER of the words corresponded with the semantic relations between them.

The third aspect of the syntactic data that was important for the analysis of the structure of utterances was the relatively small set of semantic relationships that were identified in the children's speech (see Table 1, Section 2.3.). It simply was not the case that any and all possible relations among people, objects, and events that occurred in the contexts of utterances were represented in the children's speech. The children talked about only a handful of such relationships — the existence, nonexistence (and disappearance) and recurrence of objects and events, as well as possession, location, and action with respect to objects. Moreover, they talked about such relations often. Some of the things they did not talk about were the locations of people, action on people (such as the dative or animate direct objects), conjoined action by two people or on more than one different object, the relative sizes, colors or qualities of objects, temporal relations of events, *etc.*

In effect, it was the convergence of context information with what the children said that provided evidence for resolving the ambiguity of their utterances. For example, given just the utterance "Mommy pigtail" one could interpret it as "Mommy's pigtail" or "Mommy has a pigtail". Children's utterances reported without context could be taken to mean almost anything. But it was also possible that different things could be talked about in any particular situation; that is, the children could refer to different aspects of an object or event. For example, given the context in which a child is eating a second cookie after having eaten one just before, the utterance "cookie" could refer, alternatively, to the facts of existence of the cookie, occurrence of another cookie, the object of eating, *etc.* But any of the utterances "more cookie", "eat cookie" or "this cookie", would reduce the ambiguity of the child's utterance considerably.

'Rich' interpretation can certainly be applied to single-word utterance data, and virtually everything reported in this study depended upon it. But rich interpretation alone is not sufficient for attributing knowledge of structure or meaning relationships to children who say only one word at a time, and the other kinds of evidence that were available in the syntactic data are not available with single-word utterances. Most obviously, the linguistic evidence cannot be used to justify one interpretation rather than another, and the potential for interpretation in most instances is, in effect, too 'rich'. It seems that the less a child says, the more his utterance is open to alternative interpretation, and once committed to interpreting an utterance, it is necessary to consider all of the alternative interpretations. Given the single word " 'nana" in reference to the top of the refrigerator, where there are no bananas but where bananas are usually stored[14], there are at least two alternative interpretations: "I want bananas" or "There are no bananas" in addition to the one offered by McNeill (location of bananas). But once the word occurs in a syntactic context, either "Baby 'nana" or "no 'nana", or " 'nana refrigerator", the ambiguity of the child's utterance is considerably reduced. And, in addition, given other instances of the same and complementing structural relationships, ambiguity is reduced even further.

Substantive forms presented the greatest potential for wide variability of interpretation and this point has already been discussed at length. 'Rich' interpretation alone does not provide evidence for supporting one underlying linguistic representation rather than another for single noun forms, and there is no differentiating linguistic evidence. Thus, it was not the case that the analysis used in this study of single-word utterances was one of 'poor' interpretation. It was certainly possible to know what Allison was talking about more often than not. Further, when one looked at all the data in the video tapes and the diary notes, it was possible to conclude that Allison was talking about many of the same kinds of things that children talk about in their early sentences: people doing things, objects being acted upon, and located in space, as well as their existence, disappearance, nonexistence and recurrence. However, describing relationships within the situation in which the child speaks is different from attributing to the child the linguistic knowledge for talking about such relationships. The behavior or interaction exists in the situation, and the child uses a word, or a succession of single words, in reference to it. But his use of such words is related to the situation (and successive single words are related to each other only because of the situation) and not derived

[14]   Example from David McNeill, *The acquisition of language*, 1970, 24.

from the grammatical 'function' or semantic 'structure' of the words themselves.

The inherent relational meanings of certain other words that Allison used were less variable than the substantive forms, and their interpretations were essentially unambiguous. It was pointed out that certain single words occurred in contexts that differed from one another in many respects but appeared to share a particular feature in common — a feature that was coded or represented by the meaning of the particular word. These were the FUNCTION forms, for example, "gone", "more", "there", "up". The relational nature of the meanings of such words accounted for their use in situations with different objects, persons, and events.

When Allison picked up a second cookie, the second cookie was "more" by virtue of its appearance after the first cookie. Because it virtually always referred to another instance (in this case, of a cookie), the interpretation of "more" was essentially unambiguous. Further, the fact that "cookie" also occurred in precisely the same situations was added evidence for expanding the interpretation of "more" in such situations, and, indeed, such two-word utterances as "more cookie" occurred occasionally in Allison's speech (see events I: 22, 25, 43, 75, 84 in the Appendix).

Verb forms also have the relational meaning component of the function forms that have been discussed — that is, particular actions involve different people performing the actions as well as different objects being affected or acted upon. Verbs like "see", "fit", "turn", "eat", "tumble", occurred in the speech of Allison, Eric, Kathryn, and Gia and such verbs as these occurred in reference to a number of different objects which the children could see, fit, turn, or eat, *etc.* Again, the relational nature of the words was an inherent fact of the 'meanings' of the words — one cannot see without seeing something, one cannot eat without eating something, there can be no tumbling without something falling, *etc.* That such verbs as these occurred in situations with observable actors, persons affected, or objects is obvious — they could not otherwise occur. It would simply be unnecessary and presumptuous to say that their occurrence depended upon, or in some way indicated, an expanded underlying semantic or syntactic 'structure'.

Two questions precipitated the study of single-word utterances reported here: "What do children appear to know about linguistic structure before the use of syntax in their speech?" and "Are the same conceptual relations coded in early syntactic utterances some-how represented in the earlier use of single-word utterances before syntax?" In answer to the first question, the evidence that has been presented appears to indicate that Allison, Gia, and Eric knew little about semantic or syntactic structure, but they knew far more about the interactions among people, objects, and events in the real world in this period of time. In answer to the second question, it is impor-tant that the conceptual relations coded in early sentences (Table 1) appear to be similar to many of the conceptual notions that could be identified in Allison's single-word utterances — particularly in her use of FUNCTION forms, different uses of person NAMES, and, somewhat later, VERB forms. Further, the occurrence of successive single-word utterances in the transition from single-words to syntax was taken as evidence of a conceptual representation of the relations among objects and events that would be mapped onto longer utterances when she succeeded in learning the code. This leads, then, to a third question: "Was there a sequence in which expression of such different conceptual notions developed in the period of time from 9 to 21 months?"

It certainly makes sense that children would perceive and organize what they see and do in a coherent way with certain sequential priorities that depend upon their developing cognitive capacities. Part of such a sequence in conceptual development in the second year has been suggested here. Relational FUNCTION forms occurred earlier, persisted, and were used more often than the SUBSTANTIVE forms, which came to predominate in the last half of the second year — apparently tied to the achievement of object constancy. Thus the notions coded by such function forms — existence, non-existence, disappearance, cessation, 'upness', recurrence — were part of her experience before certain other relations among persons, objects and events — such as possession, location, action, and attribution. A possible sequence could be proposed for the occurrence of FUNCTIONAL notions, based only on the order of appearance of the particular words in Allison's speech: "away", "gone", "no", and "stop" appeared before "there"; "more" appeared after these. However, while there may appear to be an elementary logic to this sequence, it does not seem to be a necessary sequence, and there may well be alternative sequences among different children. For example, it is reasonable that the notion of recurrence might lead a child to the cognizance of nonexistence. Leopold reported the active use of [dɛ] and then [da] as the demonstrative ("there"), from age 10 months; and "mehr" ("more") at 1 year, 5 months, before "alle" ("gone", "empty") at 1 year, 7 months. It is also the case that the sequence in which particular words are observed in a child's speech may not necessarily reflect the sequence in which he has come to realize the notions underlying the words. That is, he may have developed one or another conceptual notion without having learned a word for representing it until after he learns a word that codes a notion acquired later.

When the conceptual notions are so conveniently tied to the actual words in the child's speech, such as "more", "no", and "away", it is possible to trace their order of appearance. It was possible to identify the regularities of experience to which such words referred so that they were essentially unambiguous in use and in apparent semantic intention. However, recurring contexts and regularities in the use of substantive words could not define any of the conceptual notions discussed. The use of such words as "chair" occurred in contexts of different chairs that indicated a conceptual summary representation of objects that were chair-like. In this sense, the use of such words — to refer to chairs, bananas, shoes, *etc.* — was also unambiguous. However, the conceptual notions of possession, location, attribution, agency, *etc.* were not so conveniently 'named' by any such word but, rather, would have to be inferred somehow, from the situation in which the words occurred (by the investigator, and by the child as well).

What kinds of evidence would one need to obtain in order to determine a sequence in the development of the conceptual notions that lead a child to discover the semantic-syntactic relations among words? The answer to this question is not at all clear at the present time. Thus far we have looked at what a few children say and the behavior and context that accompany their utterances insofar as such information is relevant for interpreting the utterances. Such evidence as has so far been presented has not, as yet, led to any unequivocal sequence, primarily because of the problems of ambiguity that have been pointed out. Also, we do not have enough well-documented evidence — that is, VISUAL and AUDITORY records over long periods of time, to study changes in speech relative to different situations.

Finally, the actual words that have been discussed would not have to be used by the child in order for him to have learned the corresponding conceptual distinctions. There is no reason that I can see why a child would need to say the words (or, perhaps, even know the words) which represent such notions in order to have an awareness or realization of such aspects of his nonlinguistic environment. The fact that Allison did use single-word utterances for a period of approximately one year made it relatively easy to describe the appearance of particular words and development in her use of words over time. But I do not believe that her saying or even 'knowing' the words "there", "away", and "more" was a necessary condition for her becoming aware of the existence, disappearance, and recurrence of objects and events in her environment. Her use of the words provided evidence of such awareness, and was dependent upon it, but was probably not necessary. And, indeed, there are children who reportedly use few words at all in their first two years, and who seem to learn to use sentences relatively quickly after the age of two years. However, they are undoubtedly THINKING. And that is really what language development in the first two years appears to be about.

REFERENCES

Bellugi, Ursula, and Roger Brown (eds.), *The acquisition of language*, monograph of the Society for Research in Child Development, 29, 1964.

Bever, Thomas G., Jerry A. Fodor, and William Weksel, "On the acquisition of syntax: A critique of 'Contextual generalization'", *Psychological Review*, 72, 1965, 467-482.

Bloch, Oscar, "Premiers stades du langage de l'enfant", *Journal de Psychologie*, 18, 1921, 693-712.

——, "La phrase dans le langage de l'enfant", *Journal de Psychologie*, 21, 1924, 18-43.

Bloom, Lois, *Language development: Form and function in emerging grammars*, doctoral dissertation, Columbia University, 1968; Cambridge, Mass.: The M.I.T. Press, 1970.

——, "Why not pivot grammar?", *Journal of Speech and Hearing Disorders*, 36, 1971, 40-50.

Bowerman, Melissa, "Learning to talk: A cross-linguistic study of early syntactic development, with special reference to Finnish", doctoral dissertation, Harvard University, 1970.

Braine, Martin D. S., "The ontogeny of English phrase structure: The first phase", *Language*, 39, 1963, 1-13.

——, "On learning the grammatical order of words", *Psychological Review*, 70, 1963, 323-348.

——, "The acquisition of language in infant and child", in Carroll Reed (ed.) *The learning of language*, New York: Appleton-Century-Crofts, 1970.

——, "On two types of models of the internalization of grammars", in Dan I. Slobin (ed.), *The ontogenesis of grammar: Some facts and several theories*, New York: Academic Press, 1971.

Brown, Roger, "How shall a thing be called?", *Psychological Review*, 65, 1958, 14-21.

——, *Social Psychology*, New York: The Free Press, 1965.

——, *A first language, stage I: Semantic and grammatical relations*, Harvard University, in prep.

Brown, Roger, and Ursula Bellugi, "Three processes in the child's acquisition of syntax", *Harvard Educational Review*, 34, 1964, 133-151.

Carroll, John B., *Language and thought*, Englewood Cliffs, N.J.: Prentice-Hall, 1964.

Chomsky, Noam, *Aspects of the theory of syntax*, Cambridge, Mass.: The M.I.T. Press, 1965.

——, *Language and mind*, New York: Harcourt, Brace and World, 1968.

——, "Deep structure, surface structure and semantic interpretation", in Danny Steinberg and Leon A. Jakobovits (eds.), *Semantics: An interdisciplinary reader in philosophy, linguistics and psychology*, New York: Cambridge University Press, 1971.

deLaguna, Grace, *Speech: Its function and development*, 1927; Bloomington, Ind.: Indiana University Press, 1963.

Fernald, Charles, "Children's active and passive knowledge of syntax", paper presented to the Midwestern Psychological Association, 1970.

Fillmore, Charles, "The case for case", in Emmon Bach and Robert Harms (eds.), *Universals in linguistic theory*, New York: Holt, Rinehart and Winston, 1968.

Fodor, Jerry A. and M. Garrett, "Some reflections on competence and performance", in John Lyons and Roger Wales (eds.), *Psycholinguistics papers*, Edinburgh: Edinburgh University Press, 1966.

Fraser, Colin, Ursula Bellugi, and Roger Brown, "Control of grammar in imitation, comprehension and production", *Journal of Verbal Learning and Verbal Behavior*, 2, 1963, 121-135.

Greenfield, Patricia, Joshua Smith, and Bernice Laufer, "Communication and the Beginnings of Language: The development of semantic structure in one-word speech and beyond", draft, 1972.

Guillaume, Paul, "Les débuts de la phrase dans le langage de l'enfant", *Journal de Psychologie*, 24, 1927, 1-25.

Huttenlocher, Janellen, and Susan Strauss, "Comprehension and a statement's relation to the situation it describes", *Journal of Verbal Learning and Verbal Behavior*, 7, 1968, 300-304.

Huttenlocher, Janellen. and Susan Weiner, "Comprehension of instructions in varying contexts", *Cognitive Psychology*, 2, 1971, 369-385.

Huxley, Renira, "Discussion", in John Lyons and Roger Wales (eds.), *Psycholinguistics papers*, Edinburgh: Edinburgh University Press, 1966.

Ingram, David, "Transitivity in child language", *Language*, 47, 1971, 888-910.

Jakobson, Roman, *Child language, aphasia and phonological universals*, The Hague: Mouton, 1968.

Katz, Jerrold, and Paul Postal, *An integrated theory of linguistic descriptions*, Cambridge, Mass.: The M.I.T. Press, 1964.

Lahey, Margaret, "The role of prosody and syntactic markers in children's comprehension of spoken sentences", doctoral dissertation, Teachers College, Columbia University, 1972.

Lakoff, George, "Instrumental adverbs and the concept of deep structure", *Foundations of Language*, 4, 1968, 4-29.

Lenneberg, Eric, *Biological foundations of language*, New York: John Wiley & Sons, 1967.

Leopold, Werner, *Speech development of a bilingual child*, Evanston, Ill.: Northwestern University Press, 1939-1949, 4 vols.

Lewis, M. M., *Infant speech, a study of the beginnings of language*, New York: Humanities Press, 1951.

——, *How children learn to speak*, New York: Basic Books, 1959.

——, *Language, thought and personality*, New York: Basic Books, 1963.

Lovell, K. and E. M. Dixon, "The growth of the control of grammar in imitation, comprehension and production", *Journal of Child Psychology and Psychiatry*, 8, 1967, 31-39.

McCarthy, Dorothea, "Language development", in W. S. Monroe (ed.), *Encyclopedia of Educational Research*, 1950.

——, "Language development in children", in Leonard Carmichael (ed.), *Manual of Child Psychology*, New York: John Wiley & Sons, 1954.

McNeill, David, "Developmental psycholinguistics", in Frank Smith and George A. Miller (eds.), *The genesis of language*, Cambridge, Mass.: The M.I.T. Press, 1966.

——, *The acquisition of language: The study of developmental psycholinguistics*, New York: Harper and Row, 1970.

Menyuk, Paula, *Sentences children use*, Cambridge, Mass.: The M.I.T. Press, 1969.

——, *The acquisition and development of language*, Englewood Cliffs, N.J.: Prentice-Hall, 1971.

Miller, Wick, and Susan Ervin, "The development of grammar in child language", in Ursula Bellugi and Roger Brown (eds.), *The acquisition of language*, monograph of the Society for Research in Child Development, 29, 1964.

Piaget, Jean, *Play, dreams and imitation in childhood*, New York: W. W. Norton, 1951.

——, *The construction of reality in the child*, New York: Basic Books, 1954.

——, *Psychology of intelligence*, Paterson, N. J.: Littlefield, Adams, 1960.

Sapir, Edward, *Language*, New York: Harcourt, Brace and World, 1921.

Schlesinger, I. M., "Production of utterances and language acquisition", in Dan I. Slobin (ed.), *The ontogenesis of grammar: Some facts and several theories*, New York: Academic Press, 1971.

Shipley, Elizabeth, Carlota Smith, and Lila Gleitman, "A study in the acquisition of language: Free responses to commands", *Language*, 45, 1969, 322-342.

Sinclair, Hermina, "The transition from sensory-motor behavior to symbolic activity, *Interchange*, 1, 1970, 119-126.

Smith, Carlota, "An experimental approach to children's linguistic competence", in John R. Hayes (ed.), *Cognition and the development of language*, New York: John Wiley & Sons, 1970.

Smith, Joshua, "The development and structure of holophrases", unpub. thesis, Harvard University, 1970.

Smith, Kirk, and Martin D. S. Braine, "Artificial language learning and language acquisition", in Thomas G. Bever and William Weksel (eds.), *The structure and psychology of language*, Vol. 2, New York: Harcourt, Brace and World, in press.

Spitz, René, *The first year of life*, New York: International Universities Press, 1965.

Vygotsky, Lev, *Language and thought*, Cambridge, Mass.: The M.I.T. Press, 1962.

Watt, William C., "On two hypotheses concerning psycholinguistics", in John R. Hayes (ed.), *Cognition and the development of language*, New York: John Wiley & Sons, 1970.

Weiner, Susan, "'More' and 'Less': The study of a comparative dimension", doctoral dissertation, Columbia University, 1971.

Weir, Ruth, "Some questions on the child's learning of phonology", in Frank Smith and George A. Miller (eds.), *The genesis of language*, Cambridge, Mass.: The M.I.T. Press, 1966.

Werner, Heinz, *Comparative psychology of mental development*, New York: Science Editions, Inc., 1948.

Werner, Heinz and Bernard Kaplan, *Symbol formation*, New York: John Wiley & Sons, 1963.

APPENDIX

1. METHODS AND MATERIALS FOR VIDEO TAPE RECORDING

All of the video recordings took place in the Audio-Visual Studio at Teachers College, Columbia University. They were made using a Sony one-half inch helical scan recorder, Model CV 2200.

The setting consisted of three pieces of furniture and a rug in front of a blank wall. There was a big wooden Windsor-type double chair that could seat two people comfortably. This is referred to as the "big chair" in the transcription and it was center stage. To the right of it was a child-size molded plastic chair, and between the two chairs was a triangular low table.

Three simultaneous microphones were used in each session; the models varied from session to session, but their placement was as follows: (1) on the low table between the chairs or on the floor, depending upon where the action was; (2) attached to a lavaliere around my neck; and (3) attached to an adjustable overhead boom arm that was maneuvered vertically and horizontally, again depending on Allison's movements. The photographer was instructed to focus the camera on Allison's activity — on what she was doing and what she was looking at. Virtually all of the film takes in Allison in full view.

Each session included a snack with cookies, a container of apple juice and several paper cups. A group of toys was brought to all of the sessions, and only the doll, a floppy rag doll, was Allison's own toy. The other toys were borrowed from the Speech and Hearing Center at Teachers College, and Allison knew them only in the context of the recording sessions: a metal dump truck about 12 inches long, a set of rubber farm animals (bull, cow, calf, horse, colt, lamb and pig). Other toys were used in one or another of the sessions, but not in all of them. These included a jar of bubble liquid, a group of hand and finger puppets, a 5-inch plastic doll wrapped in a blanket and a photograph of a girl in a plastic frame. The snack was carried in a canvas tote bag ("the bag") which was Allison's own and which also contained an extra diaper and napkins.

Allison gave every indication of being relaxed and comfortable in the recording sessions. There was one aborted session, however, approximately two weeks before the second session, in which Allison was distressed and uncooperative. That tape was erased. The four tapes presented here were each filmed continuously from start to finish; there was no stopping, and they have not been edited. Each session lasted 40 minutes.

My interaction with Allison could be described as somewhat more investigator than mother. I tended to follow her lead and to respond to what she said or did. I waited for an utterance when there was a hint that something might be said. I waited for Allison to ask for help, rather than assisting as soon as she had a problem (for example, extracting a cookie from a plastic bag, or putting the doll upright on the truck). I frequently asked a quizzical "What?" or "Hm?" to encourage her to say more. I also frequently repeated what I thought she had said and, interestingly, I often misheard her. There were a few 'set up' situations — instances in which I asked a leading question, for example, at 19,2 when I asked her to distin-guish between the big and little chairs and the big and little cows. Nevertheless, there was considerable touching, smiling and nose wiping. We both enjoyed the sessions.

The video recordings were transcribed originally, with description of context, by Lois Hood, who also did the original word counts. One year later, the recordings and the first transcription were reviewed and compared by Lois Hood, Patsy Lightbown, Maxine Kenin and Lynn Streeter working in pairs, and this resulted in a second transcription. Five months later, I reviewed all of the recordings with the second transcription, working in groups of three with all four research assistants. This resulted in the third and final transcription which is presented here as the Appendix[1]. Our procedure for the third transcription included one assistant controlling the monitor play-back and describing the video picture, a second assistant reading the transcription, and myself coordinating the video and audio records with the transcription. Considerably more of the situational context was added in the final version and the final transcription took approximately 6 hours' time for each 40-minute session. Part of the reason for this was the fact that we were finding new material in the tapes — behavior that none of us had noticed although the tapes had been viewed many, many times. This experience of transcribing the material so carefully and watching the recordings so closely has made us aware of the limitations in audio recording alone, and cautious of data that are not mechanically recorded at all so that they can be reviewed repeatedly before descriptions, judgments or interpretations are made. Werner Leopold's four-volume diary and several of the other diary studies that have become landmarks in the literature are even more impressive to us now, but at the same time we have an even sharper sense of how much they must have missed.

The numbers that appear in the transcriptions represent an attempt to divide the data into speech events primarily for the purpose of reference. The criterion used for the division was essentially a shift of topic or focus. All of the events were consecutive. What has not been captured is the time lapse between and within events. There were variable pauses throughout. The notation convention is essentially the same as that used for the earlier syntax study.[2] A is Allison and M is Mama. All of the utterances on the right side are Allison's and all on the left side are mine. Material in parentheses on the left is description of behavior and situational context, and the convention used for the correspondence between linguistic and nonlinguistic data was as follows. Utterances follow

[1] The draft of the manuscript for this monograph dated May 10, 1971, contains the second transcription as an appendix. This draft was distributed among a number of people who should be aware of the discrepancies between the second and final transcriptions.

[2] Lois Bloom, *Language development*, 1970.

one another on successive lines. Ongoing behavior or action is coded in the present progressive form and occurs on the same line as the utterance. For example, the description "(A picking up cup)" with the utterance "Baby" on the same line indicates that Allison said "Baby" as she picked up the cup. Immediately previous (or immediately subsequent) behavior or action is coded in the simple present and occurs on the line preceding (or following) the utterance. For example, the description "(A picks up cup)" with the utterance "Baby" on the next line indicates that Allison picked up the cup and then said "Baby" immediately after. The description "(A picks up cup)" with the utterance "Baby" on the preceding line indicates that Allison said "Baby" immediately before she picked up the cup. Dashed lines (---) indicate unintelligible utterances. Utterances were considered unintelligible if there was not unanimous agreement among the three viewers, or, at least, two firm and one tentative opinions identifying the utterance. Utterance boundary, for Allison's utterances, is marked by a slash "/"; a double slash "//" indicates a somewhat longer pause between utterances.

As can be seen, we have not completely analyzed the material in these transcriptions. The fourth sample at 22 months, when mean length of utterance was 1.73, is the Syntax Sample. The third sample at 20,3, with mean length of utterance 1.13, is the Transition Sample (between single-word utterances and syntax). The first two samples, at 16,3 and 19,2, represent what appears to have been two different stages among at least several stages in Allison's use of single-word utterances in the course of her language development from 9 to 22 months.

2. VIDEO TAPE TRANSCRIPTIONS

Allison I: 16 *months,* 3 *weeks*

1. (A trying to get up on chair)   up/
   Up. (A grunting)
   (M helps A get on chair)
   There.
   (A touching arm of chair)   chair/
   Chair.

2. (A standing on chair; looking back
   at blank wall)   away/
   Away?
   (A turning around)   chair/
   Chair?

3. (A sits down)

           down/
   Down.
   (A touching M's hip)   ə wídə̀/
   (A pointing up)   there/
   What's that?

   What?   ---/ ---/
   You see lights? You see a light?   ---
           Dada/
   Dada? Where's Dada?
           ---/ Dada wídə̀/
   Dada working?
   (A pointing at ceiling)   Mama/
   Where's Mama?
   (A pointing up)   there/
   (A pointing to M)   there/
   There.
   (A touching M's arm)   Mama wídə̀/

4. (A reaching for microphone; holds it)   there/
   What's that?
                                            ---/
   That's a microphone.
                                            oh/
   (A lets go of microphone)
                                            no/ no/
   No. That's a wire, right. We don't
   play with wires, do we?

5. (A looking down, starting to get out
   of chair)   down/
   Down?
   (M helps A down)
   Careful.

6. (A turns, trying to get up again)   more ---/
   More?
   (A trying to get up; grunting)   down/
   (M helps A get up)
                                           there/ there/
   There.
   (A sitting down)   down/
   Down.
   (A starting to get off chair)   ə wídə̀/

7.   Allison.
   (A turns toward M)
   (M pointing to chair)
   What is this?

   Chair. Yes.   ---/ chair/

8. (A trying to get off chair)   down/
   Down?
   (A gets down)
   Down.

9. (A struggling to get on chair)   up/
   (A gets on chair unassisted; trying to
   sit)   down/ down/
     You sit down?
   (A sits down)
                                                           down/

· 10. (A sitting)   away/
     Away?
   (A turning around)   ---/ ---/
   (A stands up on tiptoes; grasping
   back of chair, looking back at blank
   wall)   away/
   (A turning around)   chair/
   (A sits down)   uh oh down/

11. (A starting to get off chair)   down/
   (M helping A get off chair)
     Down?
   (A is down)
     Down.
   (A struggling to get on chair)   up/

12. Let's see what kind of toys we
     brought today. Let's see what's in
     here. Let's see what kind of toys
     we brought with us.
   (A turns to look at toy bag)
     What's in the bag?
   (M opening bag)
     What's in the bag?
   (A looking in bag at farm animals)   horse/
     What do you see?
   (A leans forward; looking in bag)   pig/
   (A stands up)
     What?

pig/

Play? Is that what you're saying?
Play?

oh/ pig/ ---/

13. (A reaching in bag; pulling out a   [ka] = cookie/
    book, throwing book on floor, not   cookie↑/ cookie↓/
    paying attention to it)   cookie↑/ cookie/
    (A looking questioningly toward M;
    no cookies in bag)   cookie/ (whisper)
        Cookie? Shall we have a cookie?
        O.K. Let's have a snack. We'll
        have a snack.
    (M and A walk off right to get juice
    and cookies)
        Let's have a snack. Let's sit down
        down over here. Sit down and have
        a snack?
    (M and A return and sit down)
        That's a girl. That's a girl. Here's
        some juice. Here's a cup for
        Allison, and a cup for Mommy.
        Let's bring the microphone over.

14.   What's Mommy have (M holding
        cookies)
    (A reaching for cookie)   cookie/
        Cookie! O.K. Here's a cookie for
        you.
    (A takes cookie; reaching with other
    hand towards others in bag)   more/
        There's more in here. We'll have it
        in a little while.
    (A picking up bag of cookies)   bag/

15. (A has cookie bag in hand)
        Oh, now, let's save these for later.

You eat this cookie. We'll save this
one for later.
(M takes cookie bag)
(A eats cookie; M opens juice; A
watches)
    You're a hungry girl. You're a
    hungry girl.
(A points to cup in M's hand)
                                             ə wídə/
(A points to cup)
    Mm?
                                             ə wídə/
    Little bit of juice?
(A drinks juice)

16. (A puts cup down, looks for cookies,
    reaching out hand)   cookie/
        Where's your juice?
    (A gesturing "gone"; looking into cup) gone/
        Is it gone?

17. (A looking around for cookies)   cookie↑/ cookie↑/ no↓/
                                            cookie↓/ no↓/ ə wídə/
                                            no↓/
    We'll have some cookies. I have
    some here.
    (A spills juice out of cup onto floor)
        Oh, you spilled the juice.
    (A putting cup down)   uh oh wídə/
        Yeah, uh oh. Oh, we'll wipe it up?
        How's that?
    (M wipes up juice)

18. (A taking cookie M is holding)   cookie/
        Cookie. Mm, I think you're a
        hungry girl.

(A picking up empty cup and turning
it over)   uh uh uh oh/
(A puts cup down; reaching for juice)   more ---/
    More juice?
(M pours juice; A drinks juice, looks
into empty cup, squashes cup)
(M taking cup)
    Where's the juice?
(A gesturing "gone")   gone/
    Gone.

19.   I think Mommy will have some
       juice.
       (M pours self juice)
       (A picking up empty cup)   more/
       (A putting her cup aside)   more/
       (A reaching for M's cup)   ə wídə̀/
           I'll give you some more. Here. I'll
           give you more.

20.   (A puts cup upside down on top of
       can, takes it off then looks inside cup;
       repeats this; then puts cup upside
       down on can and leaves it)
           You're funny. You're funny.   there/
           There.

21.   (A taking cup off can)   Màmá more wídə̀/
       (A sticks finger in hole in can)
           Careful, that's sharp.
       (A puts cup upside down on can)
                                                           there/
           There.

22.   (A eating cookie, seems to be looking
       for something)   cookie/ cookie/

Where's the cookie?
(A holding out arms, gesturing)   gone/
  Gone.
(A sees cookie bag)

                                        more/
(A reaching for cookie bag)   more cookie/
  More cookie.

23. (A tries to get cookies out of bag;
    can't; giving bag to M)   Mama/
      What darling?
    (A finally succeeds in getting cookie
    out of bag)

                                        cookie/
    Cookie.
    (A picking up empty bag)   more/ ə wídə̀/
    (A giving empty bag to M)   dirty/ dirty/ [der]/
      Dirty? You think that's dirty? O.K.
      We'll throw it away.
    (M takes bag and puts it aside)

24. (A reaching for microphone on table) oh/
      That's the microphone, sweetheart.
      We'll leave that there. We'll leave
      that right there.
    (A pointing to M's microphone on
    M's chest)   [əjʌ]/
      That's another microphone.
    (A touching her own chest)   [dʌ]/
    (A pointing to microphone on floor)   [əjʌ]/
    (A pointing to herself again)   [dʌ]/
    (A pointing to microphone on floor
    again)
      Microphone.
    (A pointing to M's microphone)
      Microphone.

(A pointing to M's cup)   ---/
  What's that?   ---/
(A takes cup; puts it on floor)

                                     there/

  There.

25. (A eating cookie, reaching in toy bag)   more/ more ---/
                                      cookie/ cookie/ ə wídə/

(A finds doll; pulling it out of bag)   baby/
(A giving doll to M)   baby/ baby/
  Baby. Ah, is that your baby?
(A hugs and kisses doll)
  Are you giving her a kiss? That's
  very sweet.
(A pretends to cry)
  Oh, what's the matter? What's the
  matter?
(A reaching for cookie)   cookie/
(A turning toward toy bag)   mm cookie/
(A reaches in bag)

                                      more cookie/

  More cookie? Oh, darling, we don't
  have any more cookies. We don't
  have any more. That's all. We ate
  them. We'll have more when we go
  home.

26. (A reaching in bag; pulling out
    diaper)   no/
  (A throwing diaper on floor)   dirty/ dirty/
    That's a clean one.
  (A turns toward M; seems to be
  looking for something)   cookie/ cookie/
    There are no more cookies. The
    cookies are gone. Here's more juice.
    Would you like to finish that juice?

27. (A drinks juice; takes another cup)

more/

(A holds two cups together; putting
them on floor)   more/ more ə wídə/
(A reaches towards cups and can of
juice)
   Shall I help you? Shall I help you?
(M pours juice in one cup)
   There.
(A reaches for juice to be put in M's
cup)

more/ Mama/

(M pours juice into other cup)
   O.K. This is for —
(A offers cup to M)

Mama/

   This is for Mommy?
(A taking cup from M)   no/
   No?
(A starting to drink juice)   [dʌ]/
   Allison gonna have it? Then
   Mommy'll have this, O.K.?
(A drinks juice; M takes other cup)

28. (A reaching for M's juice)   Mama/ Mama/
   That's Mommy's juice. That's
   Mommy's juice.
(A taking M's juice)   Da da/
(A drinks M's juice)
   Oh, Mommy doesn't have any
   juice.
(A gives cup to M)
   Oh, thank you.
(M drinks juice)
(A gesturing "gone")   gone/
   All gone.

(A reaching for other cup)   more/
    More.

29. (A looks inside cup and spills juice)
      Oh, you spilled it.
    (A looking down at juice; looking up
    at M)   uh oh wídə/
        Uh oh. I'll have to get a tissue.
        Mommy will have to get another
        tissue. Put this away, O.K.? Save
        this cup for later. Mommy'll get a
        tissue.
    (M leaves; A waits; M returns with
    tissues)
    (M wipes up juice; A laughs)
        Oh, it's a mess, You made a mess.
        Ha ha. You think that's funny.

30. (A points to floor where juice had
      spilled)
                                              [mi] = mess/
      [mi]?
                                              mess/
      [mi]
                                              more wídə/ uh ə wídə/
                                              more wídə/
        More? Oh, we'll have some a little
        later. Hey, look, your baby fell down.

31. (A picking up doll)   ə wídə/
    (A walking to truck with doll)   baby/ baby/
    (A trying to put doll in truck)   ə wídə/
    (A puts doll in truck)

                                              there/
    (A walking to M; giving M doll)   ma ma ma/ Mama
                                              wídə/

What, darling?

Mama wídə/ baby/

Oh, what should I do?

baby/ baby/ ə wídə/

Oh, poor baby.
(A going over to truck; looking at M
and doll; patting truck)

ə wídə/ ə wídə/ baby/
ə wídə/

32. Put the baby in the truck? O.K.
    She'll go in the truck.
    (M puts doll in truck)
       There she is.
    (A pulling doll in truck)

ə wídə/ baby/ ə baby/
ə wídə/ up/

    (A taking doll out of truck)
    (A holding and patting doll)

ə wídə/ up/ ə wídə/
there/

33. (A picking up truck; holding it in air)
    (A puts truck down; playing with
    truck)

up/ ə wídə/

away/ ə wídə/ ---/

34. (A pretends to cry; pats doll)
       Oh, what's the matter? The baby
       crying?
    (A walking to chair holding doll)
       Chair? Is that what you're saying?
    (A trying to get on chair with doll)
    (M helps A up)
       There.

chair/ chair/ chair/

baby// up/ up/ up/

35. (A holding doll)
       Baby?
    (A sitting doll on chair)

baby/

ə wídə/ chair/ chair/
chair/ there/

(doll falls)

                                       uh oh wídə/ uh oh/
                                       uh oh/ uh oh/

(A picking doll up)   baby/
  Oh.

                                         baby/ baby/

  Oh, where's the baby?
(A picks up doll, bouncing it)   up/ up/ up/ up/
(A puts doll down)

                                         down/

  Down.
(doll falls; A pulling doll up)   uh oh wídə/
Want the baby to sit up?
  Is that what you want?

                                         up/

(doll falls)

                                         uh oh/

  Uh oh.

                                         down/

  Down.

                                         up/ up/ up/ up/

  Is Baby happy?
(A pushes doll on floor)

                                         down/

  Uh oh.

36. (A gets off chair; trying to get on it,
    grunting)   up/ up/ up/
      Look what Mommy has. Look
      what I have.
    (M showing a picture of a girl) girl/
      Girl. That's a picture of a girl.

                                         baby/

    (A takes picture)

                                         baby/ baby/
    (A holding picture, not looking at it) baby/

37. (A holding picture out to photo-
grapher's assistant, off camera)   there/
    Are you showing it to her?
(A puts picture down)

                                    down/

    Where's the girl?

                                    girl/

    Girl.
(A turns picture over so she can't see
the girl)

                                    no/
(A turning it back to picture side)   there/
(A turns it so she can't see girl)

                                no wídə/

    No, there's no picture back there,
    is it?

                                    girl/

    Where's the girl?
(A turns it back to picture side)

                          there/ ---/ there/

    There.
(A drops picture; picking it up)   uh uh no no wídə/
(A turns picture so she can see girl)

                                there/

    There.

38. (A trying to get off chair)   down/
    Down.

                                  ə wídə/

    Hey. Look what Mommy found.
    Look what I have in the car (*sic*).
    Look what else I have in the bag.

                            ---/ car/ ---/

    Car.
(M takes car from the bag and puts it
on floor)

Car. There's your car. There's your
car.

                          ---/

39. (telephone rings in the distance)
    What do you hear?
    (A pointing to something)   there/
    Telephone? Do you hear the tele-
    phone?

                                  Dada/
    Think that's Dada? Where's Dada?

                                  Dada/ Dada wídə̀/
    Daddy working.

40. (A turns back to chair; trying to
    get on chair)   up/

41.   Where's the little man who rides the
    car?
    (A gesturing "gone")   gone/
    Who rides the car?
    (A gesturing "gone")   gone/
    Is he gone?
    (A walks toward bag)

                                  there/
    See if you can find him.
    (A looking into bag)   away/ ---/
    Where is he?
    (A gesturing "gone")   gone/
    Is he gone?
    (A reaching into bag)   there!/
    (A pulls out man)
    There.

42. (A taking man to car)   car/
    (A putting man in car)   car away/
    Car away?

(A pushing car)   hmmm/ hmmm/
  There it goes.

                                                   ---/
(car stops)   stop/
  Stop?
(A walks toward car)

                                                   more/
  More.
(A pushes car; then car stops)

                                                 stop/
  Stop.

43. (A getting up, sees doll on floor,
    walking to doll)   more baby/
      More baby?
    (A picking doll up from floor)   more/ up/
      There's the baby!
    (A trying to climb onto chair with doll) up/ up/ up/
    (M helps A get on chair)
      Up. Uh, my goodness.

                                                   ---/

44. (A sits on chair, picks doll up)

                                                 ---/
    What's the baby say?

                                  [ɛh] (crying sound)
    Oh, is the baby sad?
    (doll is sitting down)   down/ down/ there/
      There she is. She's sitting. Where's
      the baby?

45. (A looks at photographer's assistant
    leaving off camera)
      Well, she went to answer the tele-
      phone, darling. Is the baby still
      crying?

[ɛh] (crying sound)

Well, why don't you give her a kiss?
(A picks doll up; gives her a kiss)
   Oh, she's a happy baby.
(A makes doll sit)

there/

   There.
(doll falls over)

uh oh wídə/

   Uh oh.
(A picking up doll by the hand)   there Mama/
   Mm?
(A makes doll sit)

there/

(doll falls over)

down/

   Down.
(A gets off chair)

46.   Hey, look who's here!
   (M hands A a book)

---/

   Ha! What's that?

---/ ---/

   That's the bunny rabbit.
(M moves microphone, A turns,
touching microphone)   no/
(A puts book down, reaches for
microphone)
   No.
(A cries)
(M pushes microphone back)
   Well, I'm sorry. Can't play with the
   microphone.
(A touches microphone)

no/

(A spanking own hands)   no no/
No. No no. No no.

47. (M picks up book; shows A back
    cover where there is no rabbit)
    Where's the rabbit?
    (A holding out arms, gesturing)   gone/
    Gone.

                                                more/
    (A looks away and then back)
    More. Where's —

                                                gone/
    He's gone.
    (A takes book; turns it over so she can
    see rabbit)

                                                there/
    There he is!
    (A turning book)   turn/
    Turn.

                                                ---/

48. (A drops book; trying to get on chair,
    grunting)   up /up/ up/

49. You know what Mommy has? I have
     something you've never seen before.
     We have some bubbles. Would you
     like to have some bubbles? Remem-
     ber bubbles in the bath tub?
     (A and M walk away; M gets bubble
     liquid; M sits down on floor)

                                                ---/ ---/

50. (A sits on floor, then gets up and
    walks to M; looks into jar; M tries to
    get stick out of jar; can't do it)

I can't get the stick out ---. Let's see.

                            no/

Mm?

(A turning away)   up/

(A sits down; reaching for top of jar) away/ away/

(A looking at top in hand)   a wídə/

(M has stick out)

    Watch.

(M tries to make bubble — no bubble appears)

    Missed.

(M tries again)

    I can't do it.

51.   O.K. Try again. Little bubbles. You didn't see those. Here it goes.

(A watches bubble — it disappears)

                          gone/

    Gone.

(A looking at jar)   more/

(M tries to make more)

    Oh.

(M and A look at bubble — it disappears)

                          gone/

    Gone.

                          more/

    More?

(M tries to make bubble, no bubble)

    Uh, missed!

                          gone/

(M tries again — bubble appears and then bursts)

(A looks for bubble)

(A gesturing "gone")   gone/

    Gone.

52. (M tries again, splashes A's face;
    laughs and wipes face)
        Oh, did I splash your face?
    (A pointing to jar)   more/
        More?
    (M tries again)
        Oh, I can't do it.
    (M tries again; bubbles appear)
    (A points to bubble; it bursts)
    (A gesturing "gone")   gone/
        Gone. Oh!
    (A watches another bubble — it dis-
    appears)
                                                 uh/ all gone/
        All gone.
    (A looking at jar)   more/

53. (M drops stick in jar; tries to get it out)
        Would you like to put the top on
        the bottle?
        Would you like to put the top on
        the bottle?
    (A shakes hands and then pointing to
    jar)   no [key]/
        Huh?
    (A shaking her hands)   no no wídə̀/
        No?
    (A pointing to jar)   away/
        What do you want?
                                                 no [wi]/
        What darling?
    (A starts to put top on jar; changing
    her mind)   no/
        No?
    (A drops top; picking it up again)
        What do you want?

away/
(A pointing to jar; has top in her hand)   ---/ more/
(A peering into jar)   uh oh/

54.   More? O.K., Mommy'll try to do
      some more.
      (A watching M try to get stick out)   uh oh wídə/
      I'll try to do some more.
      (M tries to get stick out of jar)

                                             uh oh wídə/

      Uh oh. I can't do it. I can't get
      them out.
      (A grunts)
      It's very hard.
      (A watching M try to get stick out)   no/

55. (M gets stick out)
      O.K., let's try it again. Let's see.
      Let's try again. Here they go.
      (M tries to make bubble; no bubble)
      No, it doesn't work.
      (M tries again — this time there is a
      bubble; A watches it disappear)
      (A gesturing "gone")   gone/
      Gone.

                                             more/

      More?
      (M tries but no bubble)

56. (A puts cover on jar)
      Should we cover it up? O.K. Let's
      cover it up and put it away. We'll
      cover it up and put it away.
      (A reaching for jar; jar falling over)   no/ no wídə/ more/
                                               ə wídə/

170   APPENDIX

(A picks up jar, trying to open it)   more wídə̀/ ə wídə̀/
                                             ə wídə̀/ ə wídə̀/
(A holding jar out to M)   up/ Mama/ Mama/
                                             Mama ma ə wídə̀/
                                             Mama Mama ə wídə̀/
What, darling?
                                             Mama wídə̀/ Mama/
                                             Mama wídə̀/ Mama
                                             Mama wídə̀/
What do you want Mommy to do?
                                             ---/ ə wídə̀ ə wídə̀/
(A gives jar to M)
                                             ---/ here/
(A tries to turn top on jar in M's hand)
                                             Mama/ Mama/ ə wídə̀t/
Open it up?
                                             up/
Open it? O.K.
(M opens it; tries to get stick)

57.   Let's see if we can try.
       (A picking up jar top)   ə wídə̀/
       O.K. I'll try again. I'm not too
       good at it, though.
       (M tries to make bubble)
       There's a little bubble (on the stick).
       (M gives stick to A)
       Can you blow?
       (A puts fingers in bubble liquid on
       stick)
       Uh.
                                             ---/
       Stop.
       (A puts stick down and puts top on jar)
                                             there/
       (A takes top off jar)

58. (M stirs bubble liquid; tries to make
    bubble)
    (A rubbing her nose)   baby/
      Mm.
    (A reaching for stick)   ə wídə/ ---/
    (M makes bubbles)
      Oh.
    (A watches them disappear)
    (A gesturing "gone")   gone/
      Gone. All gone.
    (A watching M stir bubble liquid)   more/
      More?
    (M tries to make bubbles, no bubbles
    appear)
    (A gesturing "gone")   gone/

59. (M gives stick to A, A puts fingers in
    liquid on stick, puts stick in jar; M
    stirs)
      O.K. Last time.
    (M tries to make bubble; A puts
    finger in jar)
      Sticky.
    (A puts finger in mouth)
      That doesn't taste good. Let's cover
      it up, sweetheart.
    (M wipes A's nose; A shaking hands;
    peering into jar)   no/ no wídə/

60.   Well, that's all. We're — we're not
      gonna play with it anymore. We're
      not gonna play with it anymore.
      You know what I think we ought
      to do?
    (A still trying to get stick out)   no/
      Oh, you know what else I have?

                                            ---/

You know what else I have?

cookie/ cookie/

No, I don't have any cookies,
sweetheart. Look what I brought.
(M takes out finger puppet; A turns
away)

---/ ---/

61. (A holds onto seat of chair, pulling
    herself up)   climb/ up/
        Up?
    (doll is on chair; A getting on chair)   up/ baby/
    (A struggling to get on chair, grunting)
        What?
    (A kneeling on chair)   ---/ chair/
        Chair.
    (A sits down; picks up doll; looks at
    doll; pats doll; pretends to cry; stops)

                                               no/

        What?
    (A looks at doll; pretends to cry;
    stops)

                                               no/ ə wídə̀/ baby/
    (A bouncing doll)   baby/
    (A drops doll to floor)

                                               uh/ away/

        Away.

62. (A stares off camera)

                                               ---/

        Microphone.
    (A stares at camera, then slides off
    chair)

63. (A tries to get on chair, then walks to
    other side of M; trying to make M
    get off the chair)   down/ down/ up/

Down?
                                          up/ up/
  Up? Mommy off that chair?
(M stands up; A trying to get on chair
where M was sitting; grunting)   down/
(A gets on chair; sits)
                                          up// baby/
  Where's your baby?
                                          gone/
Gone?

64. (A looking as if she wants to get off
    chair)   down/
    Down?
    (M helps A down)

65.   Look what I have.
    (M picks up cow and calf)
                                          ---/ ---/
    (A points to cow)
      I have a — BABY cow.
    (A takes calf; kisses)
      Oh, are you giving him a kiss?
      That's very nice.
    (A turns; walking to bull on floor
    behind her)   more/ more/
    (A picking up bull)   there/
      What's that?
    (A holding calf and bull nose to nose)   there/
      That. What's that?
                                          ---/
    Yeah.
                                          ---/
    What's that?
                                          ---/ ---/
    That's a big cow.

66. (M takes bull from A; puts both on
    chair; bull first)
       Here's one cow — here's a big cow
       — there's a cow, and — what's that?
       (A touching calf)   ---/
          A little cow.
       (calf falls over)
                                                  uh oh wídə/
          Uh oh.
                                                  ---/
          Cow.

67. (A looks down and picks up pig)
                                                  pig/ pig/
          Pig. Pig.
       (A holding pig)   up/
       (A turns and trying to stand pig on
       hind legs on chair)   up/ ə wídə/ ə wídə pig/
                                                  ---/
       (pig falls)
                                                  uh oh/ ə wídə/ pig/
                                                  uh oh/
       (A looking at M for help)   oh oh wídə/
          Yeah, the pig fell over.
       (M stands pig on chair)
          There's the pig.

68. (A and M look at other animals on
    floor)
          Oh, what's that?
       (A reaching under chair; picking up
       cow)   cow/ cow/ cow/
       (A trying to put cow on chair on hind
       legs)   chair/ chair/
          What's that?
       (A giving cow to M to help)   Mama/
          What, darling?

69. (A sees M's microphone, touching it) no/
    No. No no. It's a microphone.

70. (M puts cow on chair)
    What's that?
                                          ---/ pig/
    Is that a pig?
    (A pointing to cow)   ---/
    That's — another cow.
    (A iooking on floor, gesturing "gone") gone/ gone↑/
    Gone.

71.   That's all there are.
    (A looking around)   more/
    More? Want more? I don't SEE any
    more. Do you see any more?
    (A looking at animals on chair)   no/
    (A and M look for more animals)
    No.
    (A turning away)   more ə wí Dada/

72. (A walks back and forth, stamps her
    feet)
    You dancing?
    (A goes to little chair; trying to get on
    it, grunting)   chair/ chair/
    Chair. It's a little chair.
    (A on chair not sitting)   chair/ chair/ chair
                                          chair/
    (A sits down on chair)
                                          chair/ chair/
    (A pointing to big chair)   chair/ there/
    What?
                                          chair/ there/

73. (A sliding to edge of chair to get off) down/
    Down? O.K. I'll help you.

    (M helps A get down)
      Down you go.

74. (A walks to M; points to toy bag)

                                                      there!/

      What? What have we got?
    (A turns and walks to animals lined
    up on chair)
    (A reaching toward cow)   [ə key] = ə cow/
      Let's put the —
    (A picks up calf and cow and goes
    toward toy bag)
      Let's put the cows on the table.
    (A stops)
      Let's put the cows on the table.
    (A turns and goes toward table)
      Shall we?

75. (A putting calf on table)   there/
      There.
    (A putting cow on table)   more cow/
      More, right.

76. (A goes to chair)
    (A picking up bull and putting it on
    table)   cow/ cow/ cow/
    (A walks back to chair; picking up pig
    and putting it on table)   more cow/
      More?

77.   Let's put the cows on the chair.
      Let's put the cows on the chair.
    (A takes calf, starts to small chair with
    it; stops and goes back to table)
    (A looking at M, putting calf back on

table)   no wídə̀!/ no!/
(calf falls over)
                                          uh oh/ wídə̀/
(A puts calf upright and goes to chair)
(A trying to get on little chair)   up/ up/ up/
(A gets on chair)
                                          up/ up/
    There you are.

78. (A sitting down; shifting legs)   down/
       Down? Want to get down now?
    (M helps A get down)
       Down you go.

79.   Let's put the cows on the chair.
    (A stops, looks at M)
       Let's put the cows on the chair.
    (A turns to animals on table, thinks)
                                          no/
       No? I think the cows want to sit on
       the chair.

80. (A walks to little chair; getting on it) up/
       Oh.
    (A gets on chair)
    (A turning to sit down on chair)   ə down/ chair/ sit/
       Sit? Sit? O.K. Well, I'll put this
       cow on this chair.
    (M puts bull on big chair and sits next
    to it)
    (A watches, starts to slide off chair; M
    helps her down)

81. (A goes to table; picking up calf)   ə wídə̀/
    (A putting calf on little chair)   chair/ chair/
       Chair?
    (A getting cow and going to little chair

with it)   ---/
(A takes calf off chair; goes back to
table with calf and cow; puts calf
down)
(A picking up pig)   pig/ pig/ pig/
  The pig?
(A still holding pig, pointing with the
hand with cow towards little chair)   ǝ pig/
(A puts cow on table; it falls next to
calf; A stands cow, then stands calf)

82. (A walks to chair; puts pig on it; tries
    to stand pig up; gets on chair herself;
    trying to stand pig up on chair in front
    of her)   uh oh [wi]/
    (A looking at pig standing on chair)   uh oh there/
    (A picks up pig; holding pig out in
    front of her)   there/
    (A holding her hand out to M to get
    down)   down/
       Down.
    (M helps A down)

83.   Can you put the pig UNDER the
       chair? Can you put the pig UNDER
       the chair?
       (A holding pig walks to big chair)
       (A putting pig on big chair)   down/ ǝ wídǝ/

84. (A getting other animals from table)   more pig/
    (A putting animals onto big chair)   more/
    (A looks around at empty table;
    glances at doll on floor; looks
    around; then going back to doll)   baby/
    (A picks doll up; walks to little chair
    with doll, pretending to cry)

(A trying to get on chair, grunting)   up/ up/
(M helps A get on chair)

Allison II: 19 *months, 2 weeks*

1. (M sitting on chair holding box)
   It's a box.
   (M sitting down on floor with box
   next to A)
   Shall we sit on the floor? See what's
   in it?
   (M and A sitting)   down/

2. (A points to box on floor, then looks
   up at M, smiling)
   What's that?
   (A looks at box on floor, then back at
   M)   box/

3. (A reaching out to M)   Mommy/
   What, darling?
   (A crawls into M's lap; pointing to
   microphone around M's neck)   [bi]/
   That's a microphone.
   (A sitting on floor)   man/ man/
   (A pointing toward photographer)   man/
                                          man/

   The man put the microphone on
   Mommy.

4. (A pointing to box)   box/
   Box. What do you think is in that
   box?
   (A looking at box)   box/ box/
   (A crawling into M's lap and pointing
   to microphone)   man/

5. The man put the microphone on.
  Right.

             Mommy/
  On Mommy. Right.
  (A sits down beside box)

6. What's in the box? Can you open it?
  Can you open it?
  (A points to box, touching box) box/
  Box. Well, Mommy's gonna see
  what's in it.
  (M opens box)
  Oh, Allison, look what I see.
  (M lets go, A tries to hold box open;
  holds three flaps)
  Ooh.
  (A looks inside)
  (A opening fourth flap)   more/ more/
  More?
  (A sliding around box on all fours) ---/
  (A looks inside box)

7. Well, why don't you take them out?
  Let's see what they are. Oh, do you
  know what that is?
  (M showing lamb to A)   Mary/
  What's that?
  (A pointing to lamb)   there/
  That's a lamb.
  (A taking lamb)   Mary/

8. Yeah, Mary had a little lamb. Right.
  (M showing pig to A)
  What's that?

             pig/

9.   Pig. See what else is in the box.
     (A reaches for pig; holding pig; turns
     to look in box)

10. (A reaching in box)   horse/
        Horse.
                                            big/
     (A pulls horse out of box)
        Big. Yes.

11.   Mommy/
     (A holds horse out to M)
        What, darling?
     (M taking horse)   horse/
        Horse. Mm. What should I do
        with it?

12. (A looking at pig)   pig/
        Pig. Here's a pig.
     (A squeals; M squeals)

13. (A rocking lamb on floor)   Mary/ Mary/
        Mary had a little lamb.
     (A holds lamb up to M, then puts it
     on floor)
     (A looking into box)   more/

14. (A pulling bull out of box)   moo/ moo/
        Moo.
     (A putting bull on floor)   cow/
        Cow.

15. (A looking in box again)   Mommy/
     (A sees cow and calf in box)   baby!/
     (A trying to get cow out)   moo/ moo/
     (A pulls out cow)

(A putting cow on floor)   Ma-/ baby/
(cow falls)

16.   Is that the baby?
       (M helping A stand cow up)   moo/
       (A pulling out calf)   Mommy/
       (A looking at calf)   Mommy/
       What, darling?
                                         baby/
       Is THAT the baby?
                                         no/
       No?

17. (A putting calf on floor beside pig)   big/
    (A pointing to pig)   pig/
       It's a pig.

18. (A squeals; jumps upright, almost
    hitting head on overhead microphone)
    (A touches mike, turns to M)
                                         man/
       Man. That's the microphone.
       That's the microphone.

19. (A pointing to M's mike)   Mommy/
       Yeah, Mommy has a microphone.
    (A looks at hanging mike)
       That's another microphone.
    (A still looking at hanging mike)   man/
    (A pointing to someone off camera)   Mommy/
       What?
    (A pointing off camera)   Mommy/
       That's a lady.

20. (A hugging M, but looking at
    photographer)   Dada/
       Hmm?

(A points toward photographer)   Dada/
   That's a man.
   Where's Daddy?

                                            office/
   Office. Is Daddy here?

                                            no/
(A points in direction of "lady")

                                          home/
   Home. He'll come home later.

21. (A sitting in M's lap, looking at pig
    on floor)   pig/
    (A reaching for pig)   pig/
      Pig. Pig.
    (A picks up pig)

                                          [ʌm]/
    [ʌm]. What's the pig say?

                                          [ʌm]/
    Oink, oink, oink, oink.

22. (M lining up cows)
     I see three cows; one, two, three.
    (A watches)
    (A reaching for animals on floor and
    squealing)   mm Mary/
    (A picking up lamb)   Mary/ Mary/ Mary/
    (A gives lamb to M)
     That's a little lamb. Mary had a
     little lamb.
    (A pointing to 3 cows in a row)   up/ [ʌ gídə]/
     What?
    (A gets off M's lap, takes lamb and
    tries to stand it next to cows — knocks
    cows and lambs over; tries to put them
    back)

                                            [ʌ pídə]/

23.   Uh oh.
      (A still trying to set up lamb and cows)   ---/ uh oh/
          What happened? Uh oh.
      (A still trying to set up animals; they
      fall against one another, domino style)   up/
          Oooh.
      (A slapping cows and lamb, standing
      up, frustrated, whimpers)   no/ no/
          What's the matter?

                                                 up/

          Up? Well, let's try again. We can
          try again. Try it again.
      (M arranges cows on floor)
      (A stands up lamb)

24.   THERE's the lamb.
      (A stands up cow)

                                                 moo/
      (A trying to stand calf next to lamb)   Mary/
      (calf falls)

                                                 uh oh/

          What happened?
      (lamb and calf fall)
      (A squealing, frustrated)   no/ no/
          Oh, what's the matter?
      (A walks to M, trying to get in M's
      lap)   Mommy/
          Ah, honey, what's the matter?
      (A trying to climb onto M's lap)   up/ up/
          You have a problem?

                                                 up/

          Up up.
      (A walks to chair with pig in hand)

25.   (A putting pig on chair)   piggy/
      (A putting cow on chair)   chair/ chair/
          Chair.

26. (A puts lamb and calf on chair, calf
   falls)

                                        tumble/
      Tumble.

27. (A goes back to pick up cow and horse)

                                        horse/
      Horse.
      (A putting horse on chair)   there/
      (A having trouble getting horse on
      chair; M reaching out to help)   Mommy/
         I'll help. Okay, Mommy'll help you.
      (A trying to put horse on chair)   help/
      (no room for horse, A giving it to M) horse/ help/
         Help?
      (A pointing to space on chair)   over there/
         Over there?
      (M places horse)
      (A looking at animals on chair)   [ʌ]!/

28.   There it is.
      (A taking horse from chair)   back/
         Back. Back.
      (A putting it on floor)   ə down/
         Down.
      (A stands horse on floor, squealing
      with pleasure)   uh oh/ there!/

29. (A picking up calf)   Mary/ Mary/
      (A puts calf on floor)
         Is that the lamb?

                                          no/
         No. What is that?
      (A pointing to lamb)   Mary/ there/
         There's the lamb.
      (A taking lamb in hand)   Mary/

Mary had a little lamb.
(A holding lamb)   there/
There.

30. (A putting lamb on floor)   down/
(A jumping up)   down!/
(lamb falls)
Uh oh.
(A setting lamb back up)   uh oh/
(A taking cow and pig to floor from
chair)   pig/
(A sets up pig and cow, standing up) up!/
(A picking up calf on chair)   uh oh/

31.   What's that?
                                                   Mary/
Is that a — that's a cow.   moo/
(A puts calf on floor)
Is that a big cow?
(A stands up, looking at animals
standing on floor)   there!/
(M shows calf to A)
There, Allison, is this a big cow?
                                                   no/

32.   What is it?
                                                   small/
Small.
(A taking calf and returning it to
array on floor)   small/
Small.
(M shows big cow to A)
Is this a small cow?
                                                   no/
What's that?
(A touching cow)   moo/

What is it? Is it small?
(A crawling onto chair)   no/
   What is it?

                                              moo/

33. (A turning to sit in chair)   chair/
    (A pointing to TV monitor)   baby/ baby/ Allison/
                                              baby/ baby/

       Where's the baby?
    (A pointing)   there/
       There, on television.

34.   There's the baby.
    (A patting herself on chest)   baby/
       Yes, yes. Baby Allison.
    (A holding chair to help herself down)   down/
    (A reaching floor)   down!/

35. (A sees truck on big chair; goes
    toward it)
       Oh, I see a truck.
    (A picks up truck; putting truck on
    floor)   baby/ baby/

36. (A puts truck down; looking around)   baby/ baby/
    (A reaching for bag)   baby/
    (A looking into bag)   baby!/ baby!/
    (A pulling doll out of bag)   baby!/
       There's the baby.

37. (A taking doll to truck on floor)   truck/
       Truck.
    (A trying to sit doll in truck; can't)   baby/
    (A holding doll up to M for help)   baby/

38.   What do you want?
    (M taking doll)   baby/

Baby?
(A pointing to truck)   truck/
(M laying doll down in truck)   baby/
  There.
(A pulling doll up)   up/
(A trying to stand doll in truck; can't) no/ no/
  What do you want her to do?
(A holding doll up)   [ʌ pídə]/
  You want her to sit? You want her
  to sit?
(A handing doll to M)   Mommy/
  What? Can Mommy help? O.K.
  We'll have Baby sit in the truck.
(M puts doll in truck; doll slides
down)
  Uh oh, she keeps falling, honey.
(M sits doll up)
                                  there!/
  There.

39. (A pushing truck)   brrmmm/
  Brrmmm.
                                  baby/
(truck dumps doll)
  Uh oh.
(A throws doll aside; putting one foot
in truck)   no/
                                  there/
  I don't think so!
(A takes M's hand; puts other foot in
truck)
  What are you doing?
(A standing in truck, holding M's
hand)   truck/
  Truck.
                                  baby/

Baby's in the truck. Which baby's
in the truck?
(A pointing to truck)   there/
(A patting her chest)   baby/
Baby. Yes.
(M helps A step out of truck)
Wait, don't fall, please.
(A stepping out of truck)   out/
Out. Very good.

40. (A pointing to M's microphone)   man/
Microphone.
(A pointing to overhead microphone) more/
More, right.

                                         man/
(A turning to, pointing to cameraman) man/
Man, right. The man fixed the
microphone, didn't he?
(A stepping onto and off M's lap)   uh oh/
Uh oh.
(A walks toward truck)

41.   Do you think the horse would like
to go on the truck?
(A turns to look for horse, picks up
cow, then putting cow down and
picking up horse)   there/

42. (A putting horse in truck)
There's the horse.
(A standing up)   there!/
(A looking at horse which has fallen) tumble/
Tumble.
(A picking up horse from truck)   out/

43. (A putting horse on floor)   no/

(A stands up, turns toward doll near
truck)

	baby!/
(A picking up doll)	baby/
(A drops doll, stepping over cow)	up/

44. (A reaching toward duck on chair)   duck/
    Duck.
    (A putting duck in truck   truck/ over there/
    Over there?

45. (A putting one foot on top of duck in no/
    truck)
    (A taking foot off)   baby/
    (A takes duck out of truck; putting
    her foot into truck)   baby!/
    (A throws duck on floor)
        Careful, don't tumble. Whoa, I
        don't think that's such a good idea.
    (M helps A out of truck)

                                           tumble/
        Tumble.
    (A trying again to climb into truck)   up/

46.   Do you think there's another baby
        in your bag? Allison.
    (A steps into truck but looks toward
    bag)
        Do you think there's another baby
        in your bag? Go get the bag.
    (A goes to bag, pulling out another
    doll)   more/ there/ there!/
        There.

47. (A carrying doll to truck)   truck/
    Truck.

(A putting doll in truck)   baby/
   There's the baby.
(A takes doll out of truck; knocks
truck over)

                                      tumble/
   Tumble, tumble.

48.   Where's the truck going to go?
       Where will the truck go?

                                        brrmmm/
       Where?

                                        Pop-Pop/ (grandfather)
       Pop-Pop? To see Pop-Pop?

                                      no/

49.   No. Where will the truck go?

                                      boo/ broo/ brrrm/
       Brrmm brrmm. Is that what you're
       saying? Brrmm brrmm.
       (M pushing truck around, A smiles)

50.   Let's put something in the truck.
       Maybe the duck would like to ride
       in the truck. Do you think so? Let's
       put the duck in the truck. Shall we?
       There's the duck. O.K., here goes.
       (truck noises)
       (A pushing truck backwards back to
       M)   back/ back/ back/
       Back. Back, is it going backwards?

51. (A pushes truck past M, off rug;
       stands up)

                                      uh!/
       (A pulling truck back on to rug)   back/
       Back.

(A struggling to pull truck onto rug) up/
  Off?
(A getting truck onto rug)   there/ up/
  On?
(A pulling truck closer)   on/
(A standing up)   there!/
  There.
(A walks away from truck)

52.   Maybe somebody else would like to
     ride the truck?
     (A looks at M)
       How about the pig?
     (A walks toward big chair; climbing
     up)   big/
       Where's the pig?
     (A climbing up onto chair)   big/
       Big, big, right. That's the big chair.
     (A on chair, trying to right herself) there/
       There.
     (A sitting)   down (whisper)
                             down/

     Down.

53. (A grasping back of chair)   chair/
      Chair.

                             baby/

     Baby.

                             ba-/
(A crawling around on chair)   down/
(A sits down)

                             down/
     Down. Are you sitting down?

54.   Mommy/
  What, darling?

Daddy/

Where's Daddy?

office/

He's at the office.

(A squirming on chair)   chair/
  Is he on the chair?
(A and M laugh)
  That's silly. Is Daddy on the chair?
(A looking at M; crawling on chair)   no/
  No.

baby!/

Baby's on the chair.

55. (A sitting down again)   down/
   Sit down.

there/

   There.

56. (A pointing up at the microphone)   man/ man/
   Microphone.

Mommy/

   What, darling?
(A sliding off chair)   down/
   You wanna get down?
(A gets down from chair)

there/ down!/

   Down.

57. (A climbs up on small chair)
   Is this a big chair?

no/

   What's this?

small↑/

   Small?
(A points to big chair)

big/

   That's big, yes.

58. (A getting down from small chair)   down/
    Down.
    (A preparing to climb on big chair)
    Do you know what else I think is
    in the bag?
    (A turns away from chair, towards
    bag)
    I think we have some juice and
    some cookies in the bag.
    (A looking in bag)
    Bring the bag over, honey. Bring
    the whole bag.
    (A picking up bag)   bag/

59. (A brings bag to M)
    Oh, very good. Let's see what's in it.
    (A reaching into bag)   cookie/
    Cookie? I think so. Ohhh —
    (A pulling out bag of cookies)
    Look at that.
    (bag of cookies falls open)

                                             open/

60.   Shall we have a snack? Let's sit
       down and have a snack.
       (A going toward the big chair)   chair/
       On the chair? O.K.
       (M and A sit on chair)
       O.K.

61. (M shows paper cup to Allison)
    What's that?
    (A reaching for cookie)   cookie/
    Cookie.

62. (A pulls out broken cookie, looks at
    it, puts it on chair)

What's wrong with that one?
(A reaching in bag for another cookie)   more/
    More?
(A pulls out cookie)

                                                more/ there/
    There.

63. (M shows broken cookie to A; A
    reaching into cookie bag)
        What shall I do with this? What's
        that?
    (A pulls out two cookies; puts one
    back)
        Oh, I think we have enough.
    (A offering cookie to M)   Mommy/
        Oh, thank you.
    (M taking cookie)   cookie/
        Thank you.
    (A looking at cups)   juice/
        Juice?

64.   Shall we have some juice?
        (M shaking juice can)
        (A pointing inside cup)   cup/
            In the cup?
        (A picks up one cup; picking up
        second cup;   Mommy/
        holding it up to M)   juice/
            Mommy juice?
        (A putting cup down)   no/
        (A shaking own cup)   baby!/
            Baby.
        (A picking up M's cup;   Mommy/
        looking inside cup)   juice/

65. (A pretends to drink; returning empty

cup to M)   juice/ Mommy/
  Juice? Is there juice in that cup?

                                                   no/
  No.
  (A watching M pour juice)   Mommy/

66. (A drinks own juice and pointing to
    M's cup)   juice/ Mommy/
      Uh huh.

                                                   juice/
    Juice.
    (A drinks juice)

67.   What happened to the juice?

                                                   gone/
      Gone? Let me see; is there any juice
      in the glass?

                                                   no/
      No. Is it gone?
      (A crushing cup)   ---/ no/
        Oh, don't break up the cup, we
        won't be able to have more juice.
        How about your cookie?

68. (A putting cup in bag)   back/
    Back.

69. (A bites a cookie and then puts it on
    chair next to her)
      Is that good?
    (A preparing to climb down)   down/
      Want to get down?
    (A dangling over edge of chair, picks
    up cookie)
    (A getting down, turning, sitting on
    floor with cookie)   down/ down/ down/

70. (A breaks cookie)
    What happened? What happened
    to the cookie? What happened to it? mmm/
    (A burps)
    What was that? What did I hear?

                                       burp/
    Burp.

71. (A climbing on small chair)   small/ small/ small/
    More? Oh, small. Can I tie your
    shoe?
    (A looking at shoes, touching tied
    shoestring)   please/
    Please. (laughs)

72. (M tying A's shoe)   wow wow wow/ bow
                                     wow/
    Bow wow? Who says bow wow?
    Who says bow wow?
    (A eating cookie)   home/
    Who?

                                     bow wow/
    Where's the bow wow?
    (A staring ahead, thinking)   home/
    Bow wow's home? Yeah, the bow
    wow is home. We didn't bring the
    bow wow.

73. (A playing with cookie)   baby!/
    Where's the baby?

                                     home/ bow wow/ bow
                                     wow/
    Bow wow. Who says bow wow?

                                     home/
    Does the baby say bow wow?

                                     no/

No. Does the cat say bow wow?

no/

Who says bow wow?

baby/ baby/

Does the baby say bow wow?

no/

Does the dog say bow wow? Does
the dog say bow wow?
(A does not answer; smiles and grunts)

mm/

(M laughs)

74. (A gives cookie to M)

no/

You don't want that cookie.
(A sliding from chair to M's lap)   down Mommy/
Down.
(A whimpering and hugging M)   ma ma ma/
What's the matter? You want to see
what else is in the bag? You want to
see what else is in the bag?

75. (A looking up at microphone;   mmm/
turning towards photographer;
pointing; sees T.V. monitor)   man/ Mommy/
                                    Mommy/

Yes, there's Mommy on television.
Shall we see what else is in our
bag?
(A pointing to monitor)   Mommy!/
Yes, there's Mommy.
(A pointing to monitor)   baby!/
Baby!
(A pointing to monitor)   Mommy/
Yes.
(A turns to M, touching microphone) Mommy/ man/ man/

Microphone.
(A touching M's chest)   Mommy/

76. (A pretending to cry, hugs M)
    Oh, who's crying?

                                          baby/

    Baby's crying? Shall we see what
    else is in our bag?
    (A gets down from M's lap)

                                          ---/

    (A walks away from bag to table)
    No, you don't want to see what else
    is in here?

                                          ---/

    (M pulls out tiny baby doll wrapped
    in blanket)
    Look what I have.
    (A looking at doll)   baby/
    Yeah.

77. (A taking doll and pulling at its
    blanket)   off/
    Off?

                                          blanket/

    Blanket.
    (A pulling at blanket, giving doll to
    M for help)   off/
    Off?
    (M takes doll and loosens blanket)
    O.K., we'll take the blanket off.
    (M returns doll to A)
    There.
    (M turns A around)
    Turn around.
    (A pulls blanket and doll falls to
    floor)

Ah, where's the baby?
(A sits on M's lap; looking for it)
There she is. Do you see her?
Allison. She's next to the horse on
the floor.

78. (A gets off M's lap, looking around
    at toys strewn on floor)   baby/
        Don't you see her? She's right here.
    (M points)
    (A picks up doll, looking at naked
    doll)   [nu nu] = nudie/
        Nudie. Is she a nudie baby?

79. (A looking on floor)   blanket/
    Blanket? Here it is.
        (M gives blanket to A)

                                            cover/

        Cover?
    (A drops blanket)

                                            uh/ uh oh/

    (A yawns, starts to crawl into M's lap)
        You sleepy girl. Oh. you're a sleepy
        girl.

80. (A picking up blanket;   blanket/
    handing blanket to M)   cover/
        Blanket? Cover?
    (A touches doll's head)

                                            head/
    (A touching doll's head, lifting doll to
    her own head)   head/
    (A touching doll's head in front of her) head/ head/
        Head?

                                            cover/

        Cover her head?

81. (A turning doll upside down and
    around, pointing to legs)   knee/ nudie/
      Nudie.
    (A looking at her own hand)   hand/
      Hand.
    (A gives doll to M, starts to climb on
    on big chair, pretends to cry)

82.   Look! We'll cover the baby. Who's
      crying? I hear a whimper.
    (A is still climbing on chair; M cover-
    ing doll)   baby/
      Is the baby whimpering?

83.   O.K., she's all covered.
    (A turns to M holding doll)
      You know, maybe the baby's dirty.
      Do you think the baby's dirty?
      Think she's dirty? Allison, I think
      the baby's dirty.
    (A climbs down from chair)
    (A looking at baby in M's hand)   dirty/
      Dirty. Yeah, I think she's dirty.
    (A taking doll from M)   dirty/ dirty/
      Dirty, yeah, she's very dirty. I think
      we ought to give her a bath.

                                home/
      Home. When we get home? Well,
      let's pretend we'll give her a bath
      now. O.K.? Shall we give her a
      bath?
    (A 'dancing' doll on chair)   [mʌ]/
      What?

                                bath/
      Bath? O.K. Let's put her in the
      bath — put her in the tub.
    (A puts doll on floor where M points)

84.   There's a tub.
      (M takes cup from bag)
         Oh, let's put her in here, put her in
         in the cup.
         Let's pretend there's water in the
         cup.
      (M puts cup on floor)
      (A sits down hard)
         Oop. We'll give her a bath.
      (A puts doll in cup)
         That's right.

85. (cup falls over)
         O.K. Let's splash. Can you
         splash? Can you splash?
      (M bouncing doll in cup)
         Splash, splash splash, splash,
         splash.
      (A reaches for doll)
                                                baby/ splash/ dirty/
         Baby. Bath. Dirty.
      (A takes doll from cup; looks at it)
         We need some soap.
      (A putting doll in cup)   bath/
         Bath.
                                                home/
         Home?
      (M bouncing doll in cup)
         O.K. That's all. Take her out.
         Ohhhh.

86. (A takes doll from M; looking at it) clean/
         Clean, yes. Let's wrap her up QUICK.
      (M takes doll to wrap in blanket)
         O.K. What shall we do? Hmmm?
      (A rubbing hands together)   hand/

Hand? Shall we dry 'er hand? O.K.,
dry 'er hand.
(M 'dries' doll's hand)

87. (A taking doll from M; putting it into
cup)   more/ more/ more/
                                                more!/
    More!

88. (A bounces doll up and down as M
    had done; stops; holding doll out,
    looking into empty cup)   bath/
        Bath.
    (A bouncing doll in cup again)   bath/
    (A picking up imaginary soap from
    floor)   scrub/
    (A 'scrubbing' doll's head)   scrub/
        Scrub, scrub.
                                                baby/
    Baby. Scrub, scrub.

89. (A putting cup with doll in it on big
    chair)   bath/
    (A looks at doll in cup on chair,
    laughs)
    (A taking doll out of cup)   out/
    Out?

90. (A bouncing doll in cup)
        O.K. I think she's all clean now.
        Let's dry her off, dry her.
    (A giving doll to M)   towel/
        Towel, O.K. Dry, dry, dry, dry.
    (M 'dries' doll)

91.   Do you think she'd like to go for a
      ride in the truck now that she's all
      clean? What do you say? She'll go
      ride in the truck?
      (A turns away from M towards chair)
          Where's the truck?
      (A turning back to M, pointing to
      truck)   there!/
          There.
      (A stepping over toys)   up/ step/ step/
      (A walking to truck)   duck/
      (A pulling duck out of truck)   truck/
      (A bringing truck to M)   bop/ bop/
                                                bop/ bop/ (whisper)

92. (A yawns)
        Oh, you sleepy girl.

                                                bop/
        Bop!

                                                home/
        Who's Bob?

                                                home/
        Home.
      (A whimpers)
        Oooh, what?
      (A carrying truck toward bag;   tumble/
      whimpers)
        Who tumbled?
      (nothing appears to have fallen)
      (A placing truck on floor)   baby/

93.   O.K. Here's the little baby.
      (A taking doll from M)   big baby/

94. (A pushing doll in truck and making
    truck noises)   brrrm/

Brrrm. Where do you think she'll
go in the truck? Will she go to the
store?

95. (A takes doll out of truck; putting it
    back in)   there/
      There.

                                     cookie/ cookie/
      Cookie?
    (A stands up, turns toward M, looks
    around; then, pointing to cookie)   cookie/
    (M gives cookie to A)
    (A refuses cookie and whimpers,
    trying to climb on big chair)   oh Mommy/ Mommy/
                                       Mommy/

96.   What? What?
    (A crawling into M's lap)   Mommy/ Mommy/
    (A looking at photographer)   Mommy/
      What?
    (A turning back to M, touching M's
    microphone)   man/
      Microphone.

                                     man/
    Man put that microphone on, right.

                                   Mommy/
      What?
    (A pointing toward photographer,
    touches her mouth)
                                 man/
      Mouth?
    (A points to tongue)
                                 ---/
    (A whimpers)
                                  down/

Allison III: 20 months, 3 weeks

1. (M and A sitting on chair; A wearing half-zippered jacket; fingers in her mouth)
   What did you see? What did you see over there?
   (M points to monitor)
   (A looking at monitor with fingers in her mouth)   Mommy/
   Yeah. And who else?

                                                                    baby doll/
   Baby doll?

                                                                    baby Allison/
   Baby Allison. Yes. What's Allison doing?
   What are you doing?
   (A's fingers are in her mouth and she opens and closes her mouth as she watches the monitor)

                                                                    play/
   Play? I don't see you playing. I don't see you playing.

                                                               talk/ talk/ (whisper)
   Oh, talk. Yes, yes.

2. Are you ready to take your coat off?

                                                                    no/
   No? Let's unzipper it, it's very warm.
   (M tries to unzip A's coat; A resists)

                                                                    no!/ on/
   Oh, well, let's take it off. Let's take your coat off.

3. (A pointing to her neck)   up/ up/
   What?

	neck/ up/
Neck? What do you want? What?	
	neck/
What's on your neck?	
(A pointing to zipper and lifting up	
her chin)	zip/ zip/ up/
Zipper up? Zip up?	

4. Aren't you a little bit warm? Aren't
   you a little bit warm?

                                          no/

   Besides, it's not raining. It isn't
raining.

                                    children rain/ walk
                                    rain/

   Children rain, walk rain, yes. We
saw the children walking in the rain,
didn't we?
(driving on the way to video session,
M and A had, indeed, seen children
walking in rain and had talked about
it)

5. (A putting hand to head)   car/ car/
   What?

                                    car/
   Who was in the car?

                                      Mommy/
   Mommy what?

                                    car/
   What was Mommy doing?

                                    drive/

6.   And what were the children doing?

                                    walk/ rain/
   They were walking in the rain.

	school/
What?	
	walk school/
Walk to school?	
	[ɛh]/
Yes, I think they might have been walking to school.	

7. (A pointing toward camera)   school/
   Where's school?

                                                       there/
   Who's at school?

                                                       Mommy/
   Where's Mommy?

                                                       school/
   Yeah, who else is at school? Hmm?
   Who came to school with Mommy
   today?

                                                       [æ] =Allison/
   I can't hear you.

                                                       Allison/
   What's your name?

                                                       Allison/
   [æ]?
   (M bends over A to hear her better)

                                                       Allison/ Allison/
   Allison.

                                                       Bloom/
   Allison Bloom!

8. Would you like to play with some
    toys?

                                                       no/
    No? What would you like to do?
    Hmm? Let's see what toys I have.
    Let's see what toys I have.

9. (M stands up; walking to fetch bag of
   toys from table off camera)   bag/ toy/ bag/ toy/
      Bag of toys, yeah. I have a bag.
   (M returning with bag of toys towards
   table on camera)   table/
      Let's see what's here.

10. (A gets up, turns around; trying to
    get off chair)   tumble/ tumble/
                                              tumble/ tumble/

                                              ---/
    (A gets down; looking at M)   there!/
       There.

11. (A sits on floor)
                                              Mommy/
    (A looking at M who is standing)   floor/ Mommy floor/
       Mommy floor?

                                              down/ sit down/
                                              sit down/

       Sit down?

12. (A reaching and looking into toy bag) bag/ bag/ cup/

13. (A pulling diaper out of bag)   diaper/ diaper/
       Diaper.

14. (A reaching in bag again for doll)   baby/ baby/ baby/
    (A pulling out doll)   baby/ doll/
       Baby doll.
    (A putting doll on floor)   doll/ there/

15. (A unfolding diaper)   baby/ diaper/
       Baby diaper?

                                              baby doll/ diaper/
                                              baby doll/ diaper/

baby/ doll/ clean/
diaper/

CLEAN diaper.
(A tries to put diaper on doll)

baby/ baby/

16. (A holding doll out to M)   Mommy/ help/
    Mommy help?
    (A holding diaper out to M)   diaper/ diaper/
    Diaper?
    (M taking diaper)   on/
    Diaper on? What shall we do with
    the diaper?

                                       on/
    On what?
    (A pointing to doll)   baby/ doll/
    Put the diaper on the baby DOLL?

                                       mm/
    Oh well, I think that diaper — does
    that diaper fit? Does that diaper fit?

17. (A reaching for diaper)   clean/ dirty/ diaper/
    (A puts diaper on floor)
    Is it a dirty diaper?

                                       mm/
    Mm. I don't think so.

                                       dirty/ away/
    What?

                                       dirty/ away/
    Dirty?

                                       dirty/ diaper/ dirty
                                       diaper/ dirty diaper/
    Dirty diaper?

                                       away/
    Away. I see. Dirty diaper away. Yes,
    we throw the dirty diapers away.

18. (M trying to put diaper on doll but
diaper is too big)
    I think this diaper is TOO SMALL. Is
    this a small diaper?

                                    mm/
    What is it?

                                    clean/
    It's clean and it's — I think too big
    for this doll. I think it's too big for
    the doll. I think this is the diaper
    for somebody else.

                                      Allison/
    For Allison.
    (A taking diaper from M)   Bloom/
    Allison Bloom.
    (A looking at diaper)   diaper/
    Mm. Hm.

19. (A picks up doll, giving it to M)   baby/ baby/ baby/
    Put the diaper on the baby?
    (A unfolding diaper)   ənn/ baby doll/
    (A gives diaper to M)

20. (M tries to put diaper on doll)
    On the baby doll?
    (M pointing to A) Is this the baby
    doll?

                                      no/
    What's this?

                                      Allison/
    Allison.
    (A pointing to doll)   baby doll!/
    THIS is a baby doll. O.K., maybe we
    can put the diaper on this way.
    How's that?

(M wrapping diaper around the doll)
How's that?

21. Well, we can't HOLD it on like that.
What do we need? Hm? What do
we need for the diaper?

            pin/
Pin. Where are the pins?

            home/
Oh. We don't have any pins.

            buy store/
Buy store?

            pin/
Buy pins at the store?

            mm/
O.K., maybe we will buy pins at
the store.

22. (A pointing to doll)   baby doll/ pin/ baby/
             towel/ baby doll/

Baby doll?

            sharp/ hand/
Sharp? Hands? What's sharp?

            pin/
Oh, a pin is sharp, isn't it?

23.   baby/
  (A reaching for doll)   baby doll/
   Oh, there she is!
  (A starts to pick up doll, diaper falls
  off; A pulls diaper off doll; standing
  up holding diaper)   uh oh/ uh oh/

24.   lie down/
  (A holding diaper, sitting, preparing
  to lie down)   baby/ lie down/

Baby lie down?
(A lies down holding diaper)
   Oh, you tired?

                                      diaper/ diaper/

(A starting to get up)   on/
   Diaper? I'm not going to change
   your diaper on television. Diaper
   on? You've got a nice dry diaper
   on. I think you're all right.
(A squatting, looking at diaper)   more/
   We'll change it later. I think it's
   time for a snack now. Would you
   like a snack?

25. (A goes to toy bag; reaching in)   cookie/
   O.K., let's take your coat off first.
Let's take your coat off.
(A stands up with bag of cookies)
(M takes cookies from A, puts diaper
in bag, tries to take A's coat off)
   No, we don't eat with a coat on, do
   we? You have to take your coat off.
(A holding her arm across her jacket) on/
   No, no, not for a snack. Let's take
   your coat off.

26.   You can do it all by yourself. Can
    you pull the zipper down?
    (M touches zipper)
    (A touching zipper; holding chin up) up/ up/ up/
       You gonna pull it up?
    (A starting to turn away from M)   Mommy help/

27. (A turns around; touching overhead
    microphone)   mike/
       That's the microphone.

(A turns to M, touching her micro-
phone)   Mommy/ mike/
  Mommy has a microphone.

                                                 on/
  Mommy has a microphone ON.
(A turns and looks at photographer)

28.   Shall we have our snack? We have
      apple juice and coconut cookies.
      (A trying to pull zipper up; holding
      her chin up)   zip/ up/
        Zipper up? I think zipper DOWN. I
        think we'll take the coat off for the
        snack.
      (A pulling zipper down)
        Yes! You can do it all by yourself.
      (A pulling zipper down)   [op]=open/ open/

29.   I'll go get the juice for the snack.
      (M goes to get juice; A watches)
      (A reaching her arms out to M
      returning with juice and cups)   baby/
      (A looking at something) What,
      honey?   glass/ glass/ glass/
                                                glass/

30.   Shall we take your coat off and
      we'll have a snack?
      (A grasping arms of coat)   no/
        Oh yes. You know we don't eat
        with our coat on.

31.   (A pointing to paper cup in M's hand)   glass/ glass/
        Oh, glass. Yes, I have a glass.
        I have a glass for the baby. Yes.
      (A pointing to cup)   Mommy/ Mommy/
                                                glass/

Mommy's glass. Mommy will have
a glass.
(A pointing to cup;   Allison/ Allison/ ---/
M sitting, holding cups and juice)   Allison/ Allison/
Allison what?
                                             Allison/
Allison will have a glass also.

32. (A holding zipper)   zip/ zip/
    O.K. Let's take the zipper down.
    You take the coat off all by your-
    self.
    (A holding zipper; holding her chin
    up)   up/ up/
    Oh, I thought you wanted to have
    a snack.
    (A walking to chair)   no/
    No? O.K. We'll have a snack later.

33. (A gets on chair; M stands up and
    puts juice and cups on table)
    Let's play with some other toys.
    (A getting off chair)   no/ ---/ snack/
    Hm?
    (A going to table)   snack/
    Snack? Well, let's take your coat off
    first. Let's take your coat off first.

34. (A reaches for cookies)
    (M moving cup away)   ---/
    Mommy'll let you have juice, but
    you have to take your coat off. We
    don't have a snack with our coats
    on. No.
    (A touching zipper)   zip/ zip/
    O.K. We'll take the zipper off and

you take your coat off ALL by yourself.
(A holding chin up, pointing to her
neck)   up/ up/ up/
(A screams; holding zipper;   up/ up/
pointing to neck; starting to cry)   neck/

35. Well, let's have a snack, and then
    we'll put the coat back on. O.K.?
    Let's take your coat off first, have
    a snack.

                                            no/
    Yes. Come on. Mommy wants some
    juice and Mommy wants a cookie.
    (A picking up bag of cookies)   Mommy/ Mommy/
    (M takes bag from A)

36.   Allison, let's take the coat off first.
      That's the rule. That's the rule.
      (M takes juice)
      (A takes off coat; carrying coat to
      chair)   chair/ chair/ --- chair/
      Big chair.
      (A putting coat on chair)   coat on/ chair/
      Coat on chair. Oh, good girl. Good
      girl. O.K.

37. (A returns to M sitting on floor)
    Would you like a cookie?

                                            no/
    What would you like?
    (A noticing baby doll behind M)   baby doll/
    (A reaches for cup in M's hand)

                                            juice/
    Juice?

38. Here, you hold this cup.
    (M gives A empty cup)
       Want to sit down?
    (A starting to squat on floor)   no/
    (A turns around; walking to chair)   chair/ chair/
    (A walking back to M)   sit/ sit down/
    (A sits down on floor next to M)

39. (A holding empty cup; M pouring
    juice in other cup)   baby/ cup/ baby/
    (M gives A full cup; A holding full
    cup; giving M empty cup)   Mommy/ Mommy/
          cup/ (whisper)

    (A drinks juice)
       Oh my goodness.
    (A puts cup down; reaches for cookies;
    takes one)

40. (A taking empty cup from M)   baby/
    (A sneezes)
       God bless you!
    (A looking into empty cup)   baby cup/
       Baby cup?
    (A holding cup out to M)   Mommy/
       Mommy what?

          baby/

41. (A bites cookie; sees doll on floor)   baby!/ baby doll!/
       Baby doll?
    (A noticing other cup with juice on
    floor; puts cookie down)

          more/

    (A picks up cup, drinks)

42. (A reaching for cookie for doll)   baby doll/ baby doll/
          cookie/

    (A gives cookie to doll)

Baby doll cookie. Mm Mm Mm.
Is that good?
(A offers cookie to M)
(A takes another bite of cookie)

43. (A putting cookie in cup)   glass/
    Well, what did you do?   glass/
    What did you do? Where's the
    cookie?

                                               cup/
    In the cup.

44. (A takes cookie out of cup; eating it) ---/ ---/
    Is that a yummy cookie?

                                               mm hmm/
    Mommy'll have a piece also. Mmm.
    (A putting cookie in cup again)   back/ back/
    (A eats piece of cookie)

45. (A pointing to juice)   more juice/
    (A picks up second cup)
    More juice?
    (A offering one cup to M)   Mommy/
    What?
    (A looking at other cup in other hand) Mommy/
    What? What?
    (A giving cup to M)   Mommy juice/
    Mommy juice?

46. (M pouring juice into cup, A watching) Allison!/ no!/
    (A reaching out, trying to take cup
    from M to pour juice back in
    container)   back/
    Oh, you want to pour it back.
    (M keeping cup, starts to pour it back;
    A gesturing 'pouring' with her left

hand into cup in her right hand)   mm/
(A transfers empty cup to her left
hand; and repeating the pouring
gesture, ends up putting cup over her
right hand)   baby/ juice/
   Baby juice?
(M puts down cup of juice, reaches
for A's cup)
   O.K. Allison needs some juice.
(M takes empty cup from A)
(A taking cup of juice from M)   Mommy/
(A noticing juice that M has spilled)   uh oh!/
   Uh oh.
(A smiles, looking at juice spilled on
floor)   Mommy/
   What did Mommy do?

                                       spill/

47. (A's cup tips, spills juice inadvertently)
   Mommy spilled. Ooo la la. Allison
   spilling.
   (A laughs)
   (M laughs)
   What did you do? What did you
   do? (M laughs)
   (M wiping up juice)   mess/
   Mess. Yes. Let's wipe it up.
   (A watching M wiping floor)   more/
   More, yeah. Here, how 'bout
   DRINKING the juice?
   (M gives cup of juice back to A)

48. (A drinks; puts down cup)
   (A reaching for cup again)   more/
   (A looking into empty cup)   all gone/
   (A shakes cup; turns it over; looking

at wet spot on floor)   uh oh/ again!/
(A holding leg, looking at juice spilled
on floor)
  Again?
(M and A laugh)
  What's again?
(A turns cup over; last drops spill out)
  Oh, honey, don't spill it on purpose.
  That's not so funny. That isn't
  funny.
(A laughing)
(A taking cup; laughing)   funny/
(A turns cup over)
  That's not funny. You're silly. Oh,
  let's put it away. Maybe you don't
  want any more. We'll put it away
  and have some later.
(A takes cup again; pretends to drink;
turns it over)
  Oh, that's enough. You're silly.
  You're a silly girl. You're a silly
  girl.

49. (A reaching for cup)   more/
  We'll have some later. I don't think
  you really want it. I'm gonna bring
  the toys over.
(M goes for toys to table off camera;
A running after her)   no/ no/ no/
(A screams)
(A reaching for cup on table)   nonono/ cup/
  Cup. Would you like a little more
  juice?
(M lifting dump truck out of box to
put on table)   no/
  Would you like a little more juice?

50. (A reaching for truck on table)   truck/
    O.K. You take the truck and I'll
    bring you a little more juice. Take
    the truck back to the chair.

                                              brrm/
    (A starts back with truck; puts it
    down; picking it up)   wee/
    Wee!
    (A goes to little chair, then to big
    chair, then turning to floor)   sit/
    (A puts truck down; standing up,
    looking around, excited)   baby doll/ baby doll/
    (A turning toward chair)
    (M pointing to doll)
    There she is. There's the baby doll.

51. (A laughs; running to doll on floor)   running/ running/
    Running.

52. (A picks up doll; running back to
    truck with it)   Allison/ baby doll/
                                              truck/

    Baby doll truck.
    (A sitting doll in truck)   sit/ sit/

53. (A starts to move truck)
    (A pushing truck throughout)   up/ town/
    Uptown?

                                              bye/

    Bye.

                                              up/ town/

    Who's going uptown?

                                              baby/ doll/

54. (A picks up doll; makes her lie down
    on top of truck)

(doll falls off)

lie down/

(A picks up doll)
Tumble.

uh oh/ tumble/

(A starting towards truck with doll)   sit down/ more/
(A sitting doll in truck)   sit/ sit down/ sit/
(A succeeds; doll sitting in truck)   sit!/

55. (A pushing truck with doll in it)   up/ town// up/ town/
    Who's going uptown?
    (A sees napkin that truck has rolled
    over)   napkin/
    (A picking up and holding napkin)   on/ baby doll/ baby/
                                               doll/ napkin/

    Baby doll NAPKIN?
    (A opening napkin)   on/
    On?

56. (A taking doll out of truck)   ---/
    (A tries to spread napkin in truck;
    can't; starts to crumple it in truck
    and then wipes truck; takes napkin
    out)
    (A wiping truck again)   dirty/
    Oh, it's dirty?

57. (A walks to big chair with napkin;
    wipes it)
    What are you doing?

                                          scrub/
    Oh, scrub.
    (A walks to bag; wiping it)   bag/
    Oh, you're scrubbing the bag.
    (A walks to table; wiping it)   table/
    Scrubbing the table?

(A goes to small chair; wiping it)   chair/
  And the chair? You're a big help.
  You're pretty good to have around.

58. (A wipes truck)
  (A going to doll)   baby doll/ diaper/
  (A wipes doll's bottom)

59. (A picking up doll; carrying her to
  chair)   baby doll/ baby doll/
    clean/
  (A puts doll on chair; wipes her)
    Baby doll clean?
  (A wipes doll)
    What are you doing?
  (A wiping doll)   clean/ clean/
    Clean.
  (A still wiping doll)   clean/

60. (A turns and starts towards big chair;
  her foot catches on the corner of the
  rug and she stumbles, does not look
  down, continues to big chair, picks
  up her coat; carrying it toward M)   [gɪp]=skip/ skip/ skip/
    What, honey?
  (A stops; starting back towards edge
  of rug)   skip/
    Skip?
  (A looking down at edge of rug;
  kicking her toe against it)   floor/ rug/
  (M aside)
    Rug. Trip rug.
  (A puts coat back on chair)

61.   I think something else would like to
  ride the truck. See if you can find

something in the box. Why don't
you see what's in the box?
(A going to box)   puppet/
(A takes elephant puppet out and puts
it on floor; reaching toward cow
puppet)   cow/
(A picking up cow puppet)   puppet/

62. (A putting cow puppet on her hand)   cow!/ hi!/
    (A waving puppet toward M)   oh/ hi!/
       Hi!
                                          ---/ hello/
    Hello.

63. (A looking down at elephant puppet
    on floor)   more/
    (A picking up puppet and going
    towards M)   Mommy/ puppet/
       Mommy puppet?
    (A giving puppet to M)   puppet/ puppet/
       Puppet?
    (M puts puppet on hand)
                                          hi!/
       Hi!

64. (A and M playing with puppets. M's
    puppet pretends to eat A's fingers; A
    and M laughing)
       They're delicious fingers!
    (M makes eating sounds; A laughing)
    (A takes A's puppet off her other
    hand; putting it in elephant puppet's
    mouth)
                                          yummy/
       Yummy? What's yummy?
    (A holding her puppet in M's puppet's

mouth; A pretends to chew)
(A taking back her puppet) hi/
(A pushing her puppet towards M's
other hand) Mommy/ hi/
   Mommy? What — what should I
   do?

65. (A taking M's puppet off M, trying to
    put it on her own hand) baby/ baby/ baby/
        puppet/
    Baby puppet? Take that puppet?
    (A trying to get puppet on her hand) hi/

66. (A gets elephant puppet on her hand;
    putting her fingers in elephant's
    mouth) yummy/ yummy/
    Yummy?
        play/
    Fingers.
        mm/
    Mm.
        yummy/
    Mm. Yummy.
    (M holding cow puppet)

67. (A reaching down for cow puppet) no/
    (A giving M her puppet) no/
    (A takes cow puppet from M; looking
    at cow puppet) Mommy/ puppet/
    Mommy puppet? Want me to play
    with THIS puppet?
    (M puts elephant puppet on hand,
    shakes it)
    Do you know what kind of puppet
    that is? Look at those floppy ears.

(A looking at elephant)   floppy/
   Floppy. What is that?

68. (A putting fingers in elephant's
    mouth)   ---/
    (M's puppet 'eating' A's fingers)   yummy/
    (A and M laughing; M touches A's
    face with puppet; takes it back; A
    puts fingers in puppet's mouth again;
    M 'eats' fingers; A laughing)
    (A pointing to her nose)   nose/
      Your nose?
    (puppet 'eats' A's nose; A and M laugh)

69. (A putting hand to head)   hair/
      Your hair?
    (puppet 'eats' hair; A and M laugh)
      You're silly.
    (A patting the top of her head)   more/
      More? What? More what?
    (A patting her head)   puppet/ hair/
      More puppet hair?
    (puppet 'eats' A's hair; A laughs)

70. (A touching her head)   [mætʌb]/
    Bathtub?

                                     [mhm]/
    What's in the bathtub?

                                     puppet/
    Puppet in the bathtub?

                                     [ə həhə]/
    I don't see a bathtub. Where's a
    bathtub?
    (A turns, pointing but not looking)   home/
    Home. Home.

                                     home/ home/

71.   What do we do in the bathtub?

                                    bath/ bath/

       We take a bath.

                                    Mommy shower/

       Mommy shower. Mommy takes a
       shower.

                                    nudie/

       Nudie. Yes.
       (A touching A's head)   hat/ on/
         With a hat on, yes. (shower cap)

72.   Shall we see what else is in the
       box?
       (A goes to box; taking cow out)   cow/
         Ooh.
       (A putting cow in truck)   cow/ cow/
       (A starting to push truck with cow) ride/

73. (A trying to make cow lie down)   lie down/ lie down/
    (cow lying down)   lie down/
       Lie down?
    (photographer goes to adjust boom
    mike; A startled, comes to M,
    hiding her face)

74.   See what else is in the box. Why
       don't you see what else is in the box.
       (A is hiding head in M's lap; her head
       is on the puppet in M's lap)
         Are you shy? That's Mr. Yam. And
         he-he's moving the microphone.
         Are you shy all of a sudden? Hm?
         See what else is in the box. Well,
         you can see what else is in your bag.
         See what else is in Allison's bag.
         Hm? No? Are you tired?

                                                    rest/
        What?
        (A takes her head off the puppet;
        picking puppet up)   puppet/
        (A putting puppet aside)   puppet/ away/
            Puppet away?
        (A snuggles her head into M's lap
        again)
            Ah, you tired?

75.   Would you like to see what else is
        in your bag?
                                                    no/
        No?
        (A reaching for box)   box/ box/
            Box?

76.   cow/
        Cow? Do you think there's another
        cow in that box?
        (A goes to box, sitting on floor, picks
        up lamb)
                                                    lamb/
        Lamb.
        (A squealing)   ba-black/
        Ba-ba black sheep have you any —
                                                    wool/
        Yes sir, yes sir —
        (A laughs)
        What does that lamb do?
        (A bouncing lamb on floor)   ba-back/
        Ba-back. Ba-back.

77.   See what else is in that bag — box.
        (A reaching in box)   cow/ cow/
        (A pulling out calf)   moo/

(M picks up little cow)
   Oh, Allison, is this a big cow?

                          no/

   What is it?
(A trying to pull horse out of box)   Mommy/ help/
   Mommy help?

78. (A gets horse out; holding horse)   horse/
   Horse. Oh.

                         horse/ horse/

(A bounces horse along floor)

                         wee/ wee/ wee/

   Wee wee.

                         man/ police/

   Man police? What's the policeman
do?

                         ride/ out/

   Ride out?

79. (A notices photographer adjusting
   boom mike; going to M's lap)
   (A holding horse, hiding head on M's
   lap)   Mommy/
   What, sweetheart? You're so shy.

80.   What's the policeman do?
   (A lying on M's lap)   ride/ horse/
   Ride a horse, yeah.

                         wee/

   Wee.
(A lifts head off M's lap)

                         horse/

   Horse.
(A lifting horse)   wee/
   Wee.
(A throws horse)

                                                          boom/
Boom. Uh oh. What happened?
What happened?
(A laughing; pointing to the horse on
floor)   oh/
   You're silly today.
(A laughing)

81. I think we're gonna pack up and go
      home. What do you say?
      (A stands up; looking at M)   more/
         More what?
      (A pointing to overhead microphone) mike/
         Microphone.
      (A points to M's microphone, comes
      over to M)
      (A pointing to M's microphone)   Mommy/ Mommy/
                                           mike on/
         Mommy microphone on, yes.

82. (A touches M's microphone)
                                           touch/
         Touch? You can touch it.

83. (A patting M's skirt where she had
      stepped)   dirt/ pat/
         Pat? Patting Mommy?

84.   Shall we pack up and go home?
      What do you say?
      (A looking around)   more/
      More what?

85. (A picks up calf)
                                           more/ coming/
      (A picks up truck)

More what, sweetheart?
(A putting truck on floor; putting
down calf)   more/ truck/
(A reaching for bull)   home/
(A picking up bull)   cow/
(A puts bull in truck; moving truck)   coming/
    Coming?
(A making bull lie down in truck)   coming/

86. (A picks up horse; starts to put it in
    truck but bull is there; drops horse;
    picks it up and hits truck with it;
    laughs; takes bull off truck)
        What did you do? I think that's
        enough. I think we'll get ready to go
        home. Shall we put our coat on?
        Put your coat on?

                                        more/

    (A picks up horse)
        More what? More what?
    (A picking up bull; starting to put
    bull into truck)   truck/ baby doll/
        More truck?

87. (A dropping cow and horse; standing
    up)   baby doll/
        Baby doll?
    (A going to doll lying on small chair) wipe/
    (A seems about to pick up doll)   ah!/
    (A suddenly turning away from doll) nap/ (= napkin)
        Nap? Is she taking a nap?
    (A walks to napkin on floor, picking
    it up)   ah!/
        Oh, the napkin.
    (A taking napkin back to doll)   ---/
    (A wipes doll's bottom several times)

wiping/

Oh, you're wiping her.

88. (A bringing doll and napkin to M)   Mommy/ wiping/
                                               Mommy you wiping/

    Mommy you wiping?
    (M wipes doll)
    There. Now she's all clean.
    (M playfully wipes A's nose with
    napkin; A and M laughing)

89. (A lifts her dress, puts hand on
    stomach and then pushes at her tights)
       Well, what are you going to do? I
       don't think you have a dirty diaper.
       I think you have a clean diaper.
       We'll leave it on, O.K.?
    (A picking up napkin; wiping her
    bottom)   wiping/
       Wiping.

90. (A goes to doll on M's lap; wiping
    doll with napkin)   Mommy baby/
    (A giving doll to M)   Mommy/ wiping/
                                               Mommy/ wiping/
    (M taking doll)   wiping/
       Wiping what?
    (A reaching for doll's bottom)   here/
       Here?
    (A wipes doll's bottom)

91. (A crumples napkin; wipes doll's
    bottom; laughs)
       There. She's all clean.
    (A wipes doll again; then wipes her
    own face; A and M laugh)

(A wipes face; laughs)
(M tapping A's nose)
   You're a silly girl.
(A wiping nose repeatedly; starts to
sniff as though blowing her nose)
   What are you doing? What are you
   doing?
(A 'blows nose')

                                       wiping/
   What?

                                       sneeze/
(A pretends to sneeze, twice; 'wipes'
her nose; A and M laugh)
   You're so silly.

Allison IV: 22 *months*

1. (M and A are sitting on big chair)
   (A puts one hand on head and points
   to TV monitor)

                                  Baby Allison/
   Do you see Baby Allison?

                                  television/
   On television, right, yeah.
   (A puts hand to head; looking at
   monitor)   there's Allison/
   There's Allison.

2. (A putting hand to her head)   comb hair/
   Comb hair?

                                 Baby Allison comb hair/
   Baby Allison comb hair?

                                   yeah/

3.   Who combed your hair?

                                  Mommy/
   Mommy, yeah.

(M smooths A's hair)
What did Mommy put in your hair?

brette/

Barette?

4. (A starts to wipe chair)
   Is it dirty?
   (A wiping chair with her hand)   wiping/ Baby Allison/
                                           chair/

   Wiping Baby Allison chair, mmm.
   (A with fingers in mouth, sits staring
   at camera)

5.   What were we gonna do?

                                           eat/ cookies/
      Shall we eat cookies? (A looks up
      at M)

                                           ah/
      Shall we?

                                           mm/
      Mm hm. That's a good idea. Where
      are the cookies?
      (A pointing in direction of bag)   in bag/
         In the bag?
      (A just sitting, pulling at her legs,
      looking at M)   baby eat/ baby eat/
                                           baby eat/ cookies/

      O.K. Baby eat cookies. O.K.

6. (A getting down from chair)   baby down chair/
   (A walking towards bag on table off
   camera)   baby eat cookies/

7. O.K. Mommy'll get the bag and we'll
   have a little snack.
   (M and A walk)

O.K.? Let's have a little snack. Eat
cookies. Come. We'll have a little
snack. Want to sit down?
(M carries bag to floor; M and A sit
down)

                                               eat cookie/ cookie/

   O.K.

(A reaching in bag)   bag/

(A takes napkins out)

(A taking diaper out)   diaper out/

   Diaper out?

(A taking another napkin out)   napkin/ out/

   Napkin out.

(A takes other napkin out)

8. (A reaching for cookie box in bag)   there cookie/

   There cookie. (A takes out box of
     cookies)

(A trying to open box of cookies)   baby eat/ baby eat/
                                         cookie//

(A holding box out to M)   baby eat cookie//

(M doesn't take box)

   Yes, you can have some cookies.

9. (A holding out box to M)   Mommy/

   What?

                                         open/ Mommy open/

   Mommy open?

(M taking box of cookies)   box/

   Box.

                                         cookie/

   O.K.

(M opens box; giving it to A)

   There.

(A taking and opening box)   eat cookies/

   Mm mm.

10. (A getting cookie out of box)   get out/
    Get out.
    (A starting to eat cookie)   chocolate chip cookie/
    Chocolate chip cookie? I think
    that's just a chocolate cookie.
    (A eats cookie)

11. (A reaching in box)   get Mommy cookie/
    Get Mommy cookie?
    (A gets cookie for M; gives it to M)
    Oh thank you. (M takes a bite) Mm.

12. (A pointing to M)   Mommy/ skirt on/
    Mommy what?
    (A pointing and reaching toward M)   Mommy/ blouse on/
    Mommy BLOUSE on, yeah.
    (A pointing to cookie in M's hand in
    lap)   Mommy eat cookie/
    Mommy eat cookie.

13. (A touching cup)   cup/
    (A touching diaper, apparently look-
    ing for apple juice)   eat apple juice/
    Eat apple juice?

        uh huh/

14. (M puts down cookie)
    O.K. Let's see. Oh, look what I
    have!
    (M gets apple juice out of bag)
    (A picks up M's cookie)
    (M shaking apple juice)   apple juice/
    Apple juice.

15. (A eating M's cookie and showing it
    to M)   eat Mommy cookie/

Eat Mommy's cookie? Are you
eating Mommy's cookie?
(A and M laugh)   mm/
Oh. Funny.
(A looking at own cookie in her hand)   Allison cookie/
Allison's cookie, mm.
(A looking at M's cookie in A's hand)   eating Mommy cookie/
Eating Mommy's cookie.
(A gives cookie to M)
Thank you, darling. Mm. Let's
have some juice.
(M unwraps cups)

16. (A reaching for apple juice can)   open can/
Open can?
(A pulls at tab of can)

17. (A taking cup)   green cup/
Is that a GREEN cup or a YELLOW
cup?

                                         yellow/

It's a yellow cup.
(A gives cup to M)
Thank you. Mm. I'm thirsty.

18. (A tries to get a cookie; her hand gets
stuck in box)   stuck/
Stuck?
(A's hand is still in box)   try again/
Try again?
(A gets cookie out; A offers M cookie
A has been eating but takes it back
and puts it in own mouth; this hap-
pens twice; A and M laugh)

19. (A flings cookie; A and M laugh)
What happened to the cookie?

(A looking down at unopened can on
floor)   Mommy open/
(A picking cookie crumbs from lap
and eating them)   baby/ cookie/ baby
                                                         cookie/ baby/

20. (A lifts dress up to her face)
      You've got crumbs on your lap.
      What are you doing?
      (A wiping her chin with her dress)   baby/ lap// wiping
                                                         baby chin/

      Wiping baby chin? How bout
      wiping your chin with your napkin?
      (A takes napkin from M and wipes
      chin with napkin)

21.   Shall we have some juice?
       (A still wiping chin)
       (A picks up can and shakes it)
       What are you doing?
       (A giving can to M)   shaking/
       Shaking.
       O.K. Let's have some juice.

22. (M opens can; A picks up crumbs
      from floor and puts one in her mouth)
      (M trying to stop A eating cookie
      crumb)
         Oh well don't —. Don't eat —
         O.K. Let's put the cookie on your
         Pamper. How's that?
                                                          juice/

         Juice? What shall I do with the
         juice?
      (A picks up crumbs from floor; starts
      to put one in her mouth; stops)

no eat/ eat/ [kræk]/

No eat what?

[kræk]/ eat/

23.   No. The floor is dirty, sweetheart.
You can eat your cookie. Here's the
cookie. Here, I'll pour some juice
for you.
(M pours juice, gives it to A) There.
(A starting to drink juice)   pour Mommy juice/
   Pour Mommy juice?
(M pours self juice)
(A and M drink juice)

24. (A puts cup down beside her; looks in
front of her)
(A reaching for cookie box)   ---/ more juice/
   More juice? Oh.
(A looking inside cookie box)   more/
(A holding open cookie box over her
diaper)   dump/ baby diaper/
(A looks at M) Dump baby diaper.
(A pours cookies on diaper)
   Oh. Maybe that's enough, sweet-
heart. Maybe that's enough cookies.
Maybe that's enough cookies.
(M takes box)

25. (M spills juice; wiping it up; A putting her finger in puddle of juice on
floor)
   Oh what did I do?

                             spill it/
I spilled it.

                             spill/
I spilled it. Yeah.

26. (A putting arms out; taking cookie
   box)   --- baby/
   (A dumps out cookies; starts to eat
   another cookie)
       Oh, are you gonna eat ALL those
       cookies?
                                 mm/

       They're too many cookies for you
       to eat. I think we'll put some of
       them back in the box.
   (M putting cookies in box)
       O.K.? I don't think we need ALL
       those cookies. Will you help me put
       them back in?
                                 no/

   (A still eating cookies; taking box
   from M)   dump/ dump/
   (A dumps box again; looks in box;
   dumps it again; looks in box; laughs,
   puts box down)
       What's in the box?
   (A looks inside)
                                  crumb/

       Crumb! Are there cookies in the
       box? Are there cookies in the box?
   (A arranging cookies on the diaper in
   front of her)   no/ empty/
27. (A looks at cookies on diaper, holding
   her arms out)   on!/
   (A starts eating another cookie)
       Oh, that's a lot of cookies. Let's
       have a little more juice and we'll
       put the cookies away, and we have   no/
       to play with some toys. We have
       toys to play with.
   (A looking around on floor)   more apple juice/

28. (A looks up and sees photographer)
    What are you looking for?
    (A covers face with her arm)
    Are you shy? Huh? Are you shy?
    (A laughs)
    What are you doing?
    (A peeking at M over her arm over face)   peeking Mommy/
    Peeking Mommy! You peeking at
    Mommy?
    (A lifts arm above her eyes; looks at
    M and then photographer)
    I see you. Where's your glass?
    (A looks around for cup)
    Where's your cup? Mm. What hap-
    pened to your cup?
    (A looking for it)   gone/
    Gone. Oh, I see it. It's behind you.
    It's behind you.

29. (M spills juice)
    What did Mommy do?

                                               spill/

    Mommy spilled the apple juice
    again. Oh, I made a mess.
    (M cleans up juice; A laughs)

30. (A turns around and finds cup; hold-
    ing it out to M; laughing)   hmm/
    What's that?
    (A laughing)   cup/
    You found the cup! You found the
    cup!
    (A licks fingers repeatedly)

                                             eating/ crumb!/

    Eating crumb!

31. (A still licking fingers)
    You've got a very dirty hand. Let's
    have a little more apple juice, and
    we'll play with some toys.
    (A gives cup to M; M pours apple
    juice)
    A little more apple juice.
    (A gives M cookie)
    Thank you.
    (A drinks juice; turns cup upside
    down)
    Let's not spill it, O.K.? Let's put
    the cookies away and we'll see if we
    can find your — where's your doll?
    Where's your baby doll?
    (A pointing)   bag/

32. (M puts cookies in box; A reaching
    for them)   no/ more!/
    (A takes box and dumps cookies out;
    she plays with cookies while M talks)
    Well, sweetie, I think you've had
    enough cookies. Well, shall we
    leave them on your Pamper right
    here, and if you want more you can
    take them. O.K., let's leave them
    right there and let's find your doll,
    your baby doll.
    (A trying to close box)   put away Allison bag/
    (A getting up and walking with box)   baby doll/ ---/
    Put away Allison bag?

33. (A walks around off stage looking for
    bag)   ---/
    I have Allison's bag is right there on
    the floor.

(A walks back to bag in front of big
chair; puts cookie box in bag)
    Look what I found.
(M holds doll and truck; A taking
doll)   baby doll/
    Baby doll.

34. (A running to table; pointing to toy
    box)   get toys/
        Get toys? O.K. What's that on the
        floor? What did I put down there?
    (A looking at truck on floor)   truck/
        Yeah. There's a truck to play with.
        We have MORE toys.
    (A running to M putting box of toys
    on floor)   toys!/

35. (A opening toy box)   toys/ toy/ open box/
                                        open/
    (A picking up horse from box with
    animals including cow)   horse cow/
        Is that a cow?
    (A drops horse)

                                        horse/
        Horse.
    (A picking up horse)   moo/ moo/
    (A standing up with horse)   no/ giddy-up!/
        What?

                                        giddy-up horse/
    Giddy-up horse. Giddy-up horse.

36. (A going to truck with horse in hand)   dump truck/ dump
                                        truck/
    (A trying to put horse in truck)   dump truck/ dump
                                        truck/
                                        dump truck/ dump

                                      truck/

(A finally gets horse in truck)

                                      dump truck/

37. What's a —
(A taking horse out of truck and pick-
ing up doll)   baby doll ride/
(A trying to put doll in truck; can't
get doll to sit in truck)   baby doll ride/ truck/
                                      baby doll ride truck/

    Baby doll ride truck?

                                      mm/

    O.K.

38. (A holding doll out to M)   Mommy help/
(M takes doll)
    Mommy help? What should I do?
(A goes to toy box; looking in box)   baby doll/ help baby/
    Help baby doll?

39. (A looks in box; finding calf)   cow!/
    A cow!

                                       moo/

    Moo. Cow says moo.
(A looks in box again; finding the
cow)   big/ cow/ moo/
    BIG cow says moo, right.

40. (A looks at calf)
(A holding up cow)   tiny [ku]/
    What?
(A looking at cow)   tiny cow/
    Where's the tiny cow?
(A showing M calf, holding it next to
cow, then lifting it up/   right here/

Right. That's the tiny cow.

                                baby/
(A making cows hug)   there/
(A giving M cows)   thank you/ (whisper)
    Thank you.

41. (A opening toy box)   box/
    (A picks up pig)
    (A squeezing rubber pig which has no
    whistle)   pig/ oink/ oink/
      Oink. Oink.
    (A turning pig over)   no/ oink/
      No oink.
    (M taking pig from A)
      It didn't make a noise when you
      squeezed it, did it? Well, it doesn't,
      sweetie. That pig doesn't say oink
      oink.
    (M offering pig to A)
      Want to put it away?

42. (A walking to diaper on table where
    cookies are)   diaper/ get diaper/
    (A picks diaper up; gives it to M)
    (M referring to cookies)
      We'll put these in your bag. Oh,
      shall we keep them down here?

43.   I thought the baby doll was gonna
    ride the truck.
    (A taking cookie; eating it)   no/
      No? She's not gonna ride the truck?

                              baby doll/ ride truck
                              'gain/

    Baby doll ride truck again? O.K.

44. (M 'walks' doll to truck; A laughs)
    There she is. O.K. Where's she
    gonna go?
    (doll in truck)　　　　　　　　　　　　school/
    School? O.K., Let's see her go to
    school.
    (A pushes truck; M makes truck
    noise; A laughs)

    　　　　　　　　　　　　　　　　　out truck/ out school
    　　　　　　　　　　　　　　　　　truck/
    What, sweetie?
    (A squatting on floor eating cookie)　truck out side/ school/
    Truck outside school?

    　　　　　　　　　　　　　　　　　mm hmm/
    Hm.

    　　　　　　　　　　　　　　　　　funny/
    Funny. That's funny.

    　　　　　　　　　　　　　　　　　truck/ school/
    What?

45. (A turns to monitor, seeing herself;
    pointing)　　　　　　　　　　　　Allison!/
    Allison.
    (A still looking at monitor)　　　　television/
    What?
    (A chewing, watching herself on
    monitor)
    What are you doing?

    　　　　　　　　　　　　　　　　　chewing/
    Chewing!
    (M and A laugh)

46. (A playing peek-a-boo with lady off-
    stage)
    Are you peeking at the lady?

    　　　　　　　　　　　　　　　　　peeking lady/

Peeking lady. Are you teasing?
(A playing peek-a-boo with M)
I see you. You're peeking.

47.   Look what else Mommy found.
       (A looking at bull M is holding up)   cow/
       (M puts bull on floor with cow, calf
       and pig)
       Cow! Well now, look what we have.
       (A watching M lining up animals on
       floor)   cow/
       Cow!

                                                  stand up/

48. (A pointing to horse that has fallen
    down)   horse tumble/
                                                  horse tumble/
    (A pointing to horse again)   horse tumble/
    Horse tumble. Yes, the horse fell
    down.
    (M stands horse up)
    There he is.

                                                  standing up/
    Standing up. Yes, he's standing up.

                                                  moo/
    Does a horse say moo?
    (A smiling)   giddy-up/
    He says giddy-up.
    (A pointing to cow)   cow moo/
    Cow says moo.

49. (Off camera M is pointing to the
    various cows in succession)
    Is this the big cow?

                                                  no/ tiny/
    Tiny. Is THIS a big cow?

no/ Daddy cow/

Daddy cow? Well, you know what
I think? I think this big cow, this
big cow is really a bull. This is really
called a bull. He's gonna ride the
truck. O.K.?
(M puts bull in truck)
There he is.

[jum]/ [jum]/ (truck
sound)

50.   What? Jump?
(A pushes truck)
He's gonna ride the truck.
(M presents cow)
And what's this cow gonna do?
(M standing cow on floor near truck)   wait/ pull/
Wait what?

---/ [kʌm]/

I didn't hear you, sweetheart. What
did you say?
(A gesturing with her arm as though
moving the truck back and forth)   pull/ [jum]/ [jum]/
(truck sound)

Car. [jum]/[jum].

51.   And this bull is riding the truck.
There he goes.
(M putting truck under the table)
He's gonna go under the table.
Under the table. Under the table.
(A reaching under table for truck)
Here he comes.
(A pulling truck out)   out/ table/
Out table.
(A starts to turn towards M; picking

up cookie)

    Mommy what?

    Mommy — (M interrupting A)

    What should Mommy do?

    Pull cow in table?

    O.K. There it comes. I'll take these
cookies out of the way.
(M moves cookies out of the way)
    Let's put them over here.
(M taking truck from under table)
    Here comes the truck. Here comes.
    Here comes.
(M makes truck sounds)
    Oh. And here's another cow.
    What's he doing?
(M moving cow closer to the truck)

    Wait cow truck? What did you say?

52. (A still eats cookies)
    I think you've had enough cookies.
    I think you've had enough cookies.
(A starting toward M)
    Mommy's lap? What do you want
    to do?
(A turns to sit down on M's lap; sits
down; M has no cookie; A still eating
her own cookie)

    Sit down eat Mommy's cookie? Sit

Mommy// Mommy
pull/ help cow/ cow/

pull cow in —/

pull cow/

help cow in table/

mhmm/

wait cow/ truck/

---/ cow/ [kʌm]/

Mommy lap/

sit down/ eat Mommy
cookie/

down eat Mommy's cookie? Is that
what you want to do?
(M pushes truck aside)

53. (A pushing her finger in window of
.empty truck cab)   man empty/
    What?

                                           man drive truck/

    Is there a man driving the truck? Is
    there?
    (A laughs)
    I don't SEE a man driving the truck.

                                           mm hmmm/
    You do?

                                           no/
    Are you pretending?

54. (A puts fingers in window of truck; A
    trying to open door of truck)   open/ baby open door/
    (A touching door with her foot)   step in/
    Step in.
    (A bending to open door; gesturing
    with her hand as if turning handle)   baby/ baby drive truck/
    Baby drive truck?
    (M and A laugh)
    Can you drive a truck?
    (A makes same gesture with her hand;
    smiling)
    Oh, pretty good.

55. (A moves to back of truck; squatting
    over it)   baby ride truck/
    Baby ride truck?

                                           mm/
    Mm.
    (A stands up; then sitting on back of

truck)   baby ride truck/
   Baby ride truck. O.K., you ride the
   truck. Where are you going?

                                                 school/
   Oh, you're going to school? O.K.,
   let's go. Brrmm.
(A stands up)

56.   I think the pig wants to ride the
     truck.
                                      hm/ hmm/
(A picking up pig)   truck/ truck/
(A goes to truck; puts pig into it)
   O.K. It's the pig's turn. He's gonna
   ride the truck. And how 'bout the
   baby doll? (M picking up doll)
   What will she do?
(M puts doll on floor nearer to truck)
                                       wait truck/
   WAIT truck?

57. (A taking pig out)   cow out/
   (A putting pig back in)   put on/
   (A takes pig out; starting to sit on
   truck herself)   pig ride/

58. (A puts pig in truck as she squats over
   truck)
   (A starts to sit on truck; sharp corner
   hits her bottom; A pushes truck away)
   (A touching sharp corner of truck
   with her finger)   bang/
   (A pointing to her back)   baby back/
     Bang baby back?
   (A pointing to sharp corner)   sharp/

Oh, it's sharp? Oh, I see. Yes it is
sharp.

                      baby ride truck!/

Baby ride truck? Can you ride that
truck?

                      sharp/

It's sharp. So you have to be careful.
(A putting hand on back)   back/
  What's on your back?

59. (A putting pig to sharp corner of
    truck)   pig/ pig/
    (A pulling pig back to her)   sharp!/
    Oh, it's sharp.
    (A showing pig to M; 'twisting' at its
    tail)   pig/ pig/ pig/ pig/
    What — What's that? What is that?
    That's the pig's —
    (A pointing to pig's tail)   hurt knee/
    Oh, he hurt his knee?
    (A pointing to truck)   hurt/ hurt truck/
    Hurt truck? Did he hurt his knee?
    Or did he hurt the —

                      be careful!/
    Be —
    (A pointing to truck)   sharp!/
    Be careful! It's sharp! Yes, please
    be careful.

60. (A standing up)   standing up/ cookie/
    (A stepping over toys on floor going
    towards cookies on diaper next to bag) walking around/
                      walking//
    (A looking into bag)   around/ cookie/
    (A notices cup and juice on big chair;
    reaching towards them)   more apple juice/

(A picks up cookie from big chair)
More apple juice? Well, honey,
that's a dirty cookie. That was on
the floor. Let's put that down. Let's
put that down. Because it's a dirty
one. Take a clean one off of the
Pamper.

61. (A takes a clean cookie)
    (A standing up with cookie)   there baby/ there/
    There. O.K., should we have more
    apple juice? O.K.?
    (M takes clean cups from bag)

62. Should we — Will you help me put
    the toys away?
                                                   no/
    No? I think we ought to put the
    toys away first.
                                                   no/
    No?

63. (A giving M cookie)   Mommy eat cookie/
    What? Mommy eat cookie?
    (M pours juice; A takes juice; drinks;
    M eats cookie)
    Mm. Good.
    (A drinks juice)

64. (A shakes cup; turns it over)
    What are you doing?
    (A shakes cup)
    What are you doing? Oh careful.
    Be careful.
    (A puts cup on juice can)

build tower!/
Build tower!
(A takes cup off can; putting it back
on)   build tower/
You gonna build a tower? Oh,
that's a nice tower. Is that a big
tower?
(A hits at cup)

tumble/
Oh, you want to knock — what
tumble?
(A pushes at cup on can)
Well, sweetie, if you knock this
tower over, honey, you'll spill the
juice and that's not a good idea.
Will you help me put the toys away?

65. (A holding cup; reaching for juice)   drink apple juice right
here/

(A moves truck)
(A moving to sit on floor between M
and truck, looking and then pulling at
truck)   sit down right here next
truck/
Sit down right there next truck.

66. (A putting hand to can)   --- apple juice/
Drink apple juice.
(M pours juice)

---/
School.

---/
(A drinks juice)
You drinking apple juice in school?
Is that what you're doing?
(A drinks juice)

67. (A looks at monitor; then at M)

                                          hi/

    Hi.

68. (A squeezes cup continuously)
    What are you doing? What are you
    doing?
    (A laughing)   squeezing/ squeezing/
                                    squeezing/

    Squeezing? What are you squeezing?
    (A laughing)   cup/
    You're squeezing the cup. You're
    silly. Your're a silly girl.

69.   Would you like to wash — wipe
    your hands and face?
    (M holding out napkin to A; A
    squeezing cup)   no/
    No? Shall Mommy do it?
    (A squeezing cup)   squeeze/
    (A and M laugh)

70.   What are you doing to do with that
    cup now?

                                   squeeze again!/

    (A laughs; looks up at TV monitor)
    Squeeze again!

71. (A points to monitor; putting hand to
    head)   Mommy/ comb hair/
    Mommy comb hair? It looks fine,
    sweetheart. Your hair looks lovely.
    Mommy brushed your hair before
    we left home.

72. (A pointing to monitor)   Allison/ Allison/ ən/
    Allison in what?

In television? Allison in television?
(A looks down at her dress)
    What are you wearing?

    Which dress is that?

    Pony dress. Can you show that
lady the pony on your dress? Can
you show her the pony on your
dress?
(A hides face; fingers in her mouth)
    Oh. Are you shy? Are you shy?
Huh?

ən television/

dress/

pony dress/

73.   O.K. I think we'll put the toys away
and get ready to go home. What do
you say?

    Cab?

    No. How we gonna go home?

    Car! We have our car outside, don't
we? We have our car outside.

cab/

no/

car/

74.   O.K. Will you help me put the toys
away?
(A getting up; running towards door)
    Put what away?

    Home? We have to put the toys
away first. Come help me. Let's go
quickly.

no car away/

home/

75. (A running back to toys and M)   more again!/

                                  drink apple juice again/

   Drink apple juice again?

(A peering into bag)   apple juice/

   O.K. O.K.

(A taking cup from M)   there baby cup/

   There baby cup. O.K.

(M pours juice)

   There's a little bit more.

(A drinks juice)

76. (A crushing cup continuously)   squeezing/ cup/
    Squeezing cup.

                                  funny/

    That's funny. That's very funny.

                                  ---/ (squeal)

    What?

(A squeals)

                                  screaming/

    Screaming? Screaming?

77. (A looks at monitor)
    What are you looking at?

(A hides eyes)

    Oh, are you shy? You're a shy girl.

                                  flower/

    You're a shy flower.

SUBJECT INDEX

SUBJECT INDEX

Action scheme. *See* Schema
Adjectives: attributive, 24; predicate, 24
"again", 85
"all gone", 22, 90, 92, 93
Ambiguity of utterances, 97, 107, 136-137
Artificial language learning, relevance of, 17, 130,
"away", 41, 54, 67, 69, 84, 90, 92, 93, 95, 110, 112, 114, 115, 116, 123, 140

Babbling, 62, 63, 71-72

Cessation, 92
Chained successive utterances. *See* Successive single-word utterances, chained
Chinese, 25
Cognitive: basis, 21n, 31; capacities, 13, 139; categories, 31, 117, 118, 119-123; development, 13; representations, 20, 21n, 31, 77, 80, 101
Comprehension, 12, 18-19, 56-59, 62, 85
Conceptual: development, 139-141; notions, 55, 112, 113, 116, 122-123, 140 (*see also* Cessation, Existence, Nonexistence, Recurrence, Rejection); relations (*see* Relations, conceptual); representations, 20, 29, 54, 63-64, 79, 80, 83, 112, 139
Constraints: adult semantic, 59; child syntactic, 126, 128-129
Contextual generalization, 17

Criterial features, 74-76, 83
Cues, extra-linguistic, 56-59

Dative, 24
Deep structure, 27
Demonstrative forms, 71-72
Developmental: change, 65, 110, 131; milestones, 14, 65
Disappearance, 89-96 passim
Disjunction, 24
"down", 88-89, 102

Embedding, within high-level structure, 125
Event, definition of, 39
Event structures. *See* Successive single-word utterances, chained; Successive single-word utterances, holistic
Evidence for linguistic analysis, 133-136, 140-141
Existence, 23, 24, 71, 89, 95; expectation of, 93-94
Experience: linguistic, 12, 59; perceptual-cognitive, 55-56, 59
Expressive vocalization, 33
Extension of reference, 100-101, 111. *See also* Over-inclusion

Finnish, 25
Form: correlation with function, 95
Function forms (words), 23-24, 70, 84-96, 111, 112, 114-117, 132, 138, 139
Functional relations. *See* Relations, functional

passim; different strategies for learning, 13, 115-123; transition to, 16-20, 61, 113-132, 139-141. *See also* Grammar

Telegraphic speech, 58n
"there", 36, 54, 67, 71, 84, 87, 110, 112, 116, 140
"this", 22, 23, 71
Topic-comment relation, in successive single-word utterances, 46-47
Topic-context relation, 39
Transformational grammar, 11, 27-28
Two-word utterances, 13, 17, 20-25, 113-123 passim; limit to, 124; semantic relations in, 21, 116-117; transition to, 13, 116, 130-132 (*see also* Syntax, transition to)

"uh oh", 36, 41, 67, 87, 110, 112
Under-inclusion, of word reference, 72, 83
Underlying sentence representation, 124. *See also* Sentences, pre-syntactic knowledge of
"up", 28, 29, 36, 67, 69-70, 88-89, 102-103, 110, 112, 114

Verb-forms, in two-word sentences, 21-22, 138-139

Vocabulary: cumulative versus non-cumulative, 66n, 67n; increase of, 43-44, 66, 67, 83, 102-104, 110
Vocalization: expressive, 33 pre-linguistic, 60
Vocatives, 98

"wídə", 33-38, 41-42, 60, 61, 62, 63, 115, 123
Word-forms. *See* Function forms; Substantive forms
Word-image representations, 72, 80, 84
Word-order: child's knowledge of, 36, 38, 61, 63, 121, 122, 130, 131, 135; in successive single-word utterances, 45, 53, 135; variations in, 131
Words: contrasting pairs of, 101; co-occurrence of, 17, 116, 119; frequency of, 66-68, 101-103; in hierarchical structures, 118, 132; meanings of, in terms of associations, 94-95; mortality of, 66-67, 72n, 80, 82; occurrence of, in absence of referent, 93-94; persistence of, 67-68, 72n, 80; re-appearance of, 66-67, 72n; used in opposite sense, 89

NAME INDEX